PUNKS
NGEL'S
N – FOR
SY $40

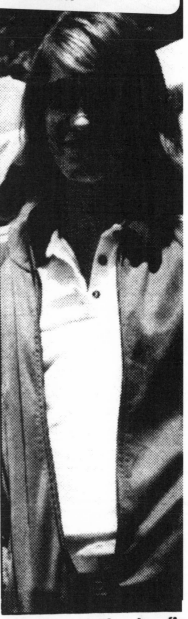

'n
as
n-
es
o

l's
n-
ig
ht
he

gs
to

Joe, a 6-ft. 3-in. aspiring musician who wore his hair shaved close to his skull, made his living working with punk rockers and taking photos.

"He was a right-hand man to the musicians in Black Flag," explains David Crouch, manager of an underground Los Angeles record store.

But the 30-year-old Joe was really just bare-

Murder victim Joe (le

ROLLINS
See A Grown Man Cry

Collected Work 1988-1991
Ⓟ © 1992 2.13.61 PUBLICATIONS
ISBN #: 1-880985-12-8
SEVENTH PRINTING

Cover Painting: PETER CUNIS
Back Cover Photos: LYNN NAKAMA &
CHRISTOPHER TROUT-HASKETT
Layout & Design: ENDLESS GRAPHICS

Thank you: Stan, Gary I, Lynn, Don Bajema, Hubert Selby &
Mitch Bury of Adams Mass

Joe Cole 4.10.61-12.19.91

2.13.61
**P.O. BOX 1910 · LOS ANGELES ·
CALIFORNIA · 90078 · USA**

2.13.61 Info Hotline #: (213) 969-8043

See
A
Grown
Man
Cry

Tired dog's legs running
Treadmill
Endless life
Shovelful after shovelful into the hole
Grey day
Weak struggle ahead
Dirty air
Breathing in orders
Half dead fish, hole in its lung from the hook
Slaps its tail against the floor of the boat
Cold eyes staring through and past
Needles in the skin, nails in the feet
Nightmares in the head, hate in the eyes
Long way down
Falling short
Falling in love
Falling asleep
Falling in line
Falling into the hole for good reason
For no reason
For real
Forever
Bullshit
Bull's eye

Sometimes I like to watch those movies
You know the ones
The ones where they believe all that shit
For awhile I believe it too
Then the movie's over and everyone leaves
Sometimes I think about that bullshit like it was real
It's what I call a junkfood thought
Not all that good for you, but it gets you through somehow
You can taste the fake truth
The illusion is poison
All of a sudden you're on your own
It's easy to get cut off
Lost in the cold moon night
You reach for the junk, the poison
You don't care if it's killing you
As long as it gets you out of this

Tonight I'm an old satellite
Emitting weak signals from far away
Low output
Where are the planets tonight
Think about the spaceman blues
Lonely on the moon
Imagine walking out of your room
And finding you're on the moon looking at Earth far away
After awhile it might not be so bad
At least they couldn't hurt you from there
Memories stick like napalm and keep burning
Years later I still burn
━◦

I'm hot
I'm heat
It's hot out tonight because I'm alive
Breathe in the smell of your body
Other bodies
The heat makes me want to destroy myself
Makes me want you
Catch fire like a disease
━◦

She went into the bathroom
She looked into the mirror
She tried to make her face smile
She hated the lines in her face
She hated the stink of this place
She hated how a man can taste
She tried to think straight
But her thoughts came out crooked
She walked out of the bathroom
Sat down and wrote a letter to life:
You bastard. I don't love you anymore, I don't love myself anymore.
I've been in the bathroom looking in the mirror, seeing the face that
sees me clearer. I don't like the lines you put in my face. I don't like the
wasted empty nights you dragged me through. I can't hang on. Does
that surprise you? You make me feel dirty. I've been thinking about you
as I burn cigarettes into my arm. It's only my flesh, it's not much, it's
a dirty hide, it's a dirty lie. Goodbye.
She put the paper and pen down and went into the bathroom
Took one last look and turned off the light
Picked up her gun and shot herself in the face

I remember the cold nights up there
Never had enough clothes
All those punks on speed
Trying to look worse than Billy Idol
Pulling it off
All those dead girls walking around
You said they were junkies
I remember the time I spent with you
You told me that my cum tasted like chocolate milk
You write me every once in awhile
You all do at some point
I like it better when you don't
I like to forget a lot these days, it's like throwing stuff out
Getting rid of you is a good thing, that's why I don't write you back
I'm vomiting every memory from my system
You make me remember
When I felt more alive than I do now
Everything we say now is a lie
We could only talk about a time that didn't happen
No one could have had it that good

I am punishing myself tonight
Three in the morning, can't sleep
I need to get out of here
Today I went through all kinds of domestic bullshit
Tiny rules for tiny lives
Tonight I'm living all their little hells
I'm going to do the best I can out there this time
I want to be that which overcomes itself
Listening to them makes me weak and small
I watch them go out and fuck each other
They tell me that I'm crazy
The years scar me
I don't want a smooth ride
I want the crushing wheel
Their glass grinds my guts
They watch you bleed to Death and call it show business

There were gunshots outside tonight
They were close
The streets here are filthy, everything is covered in spray paint
This town is a joke, a worn out paradise

It's been gang raped into shock
—+

I got thrown into a fierce fire
I found myself in a place that you had lost a hold of
I got a grip where you lost yours
I have a calming hand in the middle of a storm
I inhale the sun
I exhale the total absence of light
I am the number One
Burning
—+

She is untouchable
I wrap my arms around her and I find myself alone
She is alien
I try to understand her and I start to lose my mind
She is the most beautiful thing I have ever seen
I destroy myself when I am with her
I leave all my blood at her feet
Dreams of her rip through my head like bullets
Looking at her makes me want to rip my eyes out
She is a hollow space that cannot be filled
I have emptied myself out and caved in
—+

I want the hard nights to destroy me
I want the long haul to define me
I want to disappear beneath the crushing wheel
So little time left
Fierce awareness burning always hungry
Looking to get destroyed
Inside myself I am strong
Tonight I am napalm
—+

I got fingers digging into my flesh
I have eyes staring at me from inside my head
I don't forget a thing
I can't
It makes me want to blow my brains out
I can't explode or vomit
All I can do is burn
—+

I'm standing on the edge and looking down
Everything's on fire and glittering

I am alone and looking down and through
I come from the war in my dreams
There's a wall of fire between me and everything else
Tonight I'm walking down streets that are hot and long
I feel good because I'm alone and burning
I don't like talking anymore
I'm going to cut it out and send it to a stranger
I don't like looking into eyes
They make me feel cheap
I live inside the war reality
Glad to be all one
—◦—

I get lost in the nights
I get lost in all the stories
They envelope me until I can't see or think
All the hot nights
The glittering eyes that don't sleep
The stories the memories the dreams...
I'm standing around in this empty night
I'm waiting to get taken away
All the madness all the rooftops
All the heat there ever was in a summer night
Roaring through my veins right now
The hot nights will unfold themselves soon
I'll be wrapped in moist shrouds of solid unending night
In the dark corner of some night I lay ravaged
Glory's teeth have scarred my flesh
I've become addicted to the unending thing
Sirens of the night that scream inside my brain
The nights keep coming
The thunder screams inside me
I feel like I could catch fire
The black fever night
The animals of vision come forward
A woman once said to me:
I want to kidnap you and take you someplace special
—◦—

Road
She calls to me from a far off place in the night
My real lover and only true friend
She is long and hard and scars my flesh
She makes me vomit and hate myself

She shows me what I'm made of
She never lies
She's making sure that I destroy myself totally
I try to get away from her and she laughs
She knows that I'll be in her concrete arms soon enough
She brings me to a boil and then leaves me clawed and breathless
Soon I'll be under her iron gaze
I cannot keep away for long
Even my blood obeys her
—◀︎

The answer to my hunger is starvation
The answer to my self doubt is action
I smash hope with confrontation
Confidence is a guess
I'm here and we'll see if I fall or not
At the end of all of this we'll know the truth
The gun isn't loaded until all the bullets have been fired
—◀︎

In my cold box room
Playing the game again
Waiting night after night
It's breaking my heart
Every minute in here kills me slow and cheap
The phone calls me
Talks bullshit to me and stops
I pull it off the hook
I go outside, hear the bullshit, smell the stench
Come back to my room and sit
I'm not lonely mad or anything else
I'm waiting
Coming off the road to this place
Is like coming home to a wrecked car
It's all fucked up and going straight to nowhere
It's Friday night
What a burn out
—◀︎

Do you have the number to advance at your expense?
Do you have the number to maintain in times of stress?
Not allow it to carry over into your dealings with others?
Do you have the number to be responsible for your actions at all times?
When it means:
Embarrassment

Admitting to being wrong
Hardship and pain
Going it alone
Taking the long hard way
What's your number?
—◆—

To burn alone
To cough up blood from dirty cities alone
To see the world pass by through high speed windows
Makes me feel that finally I'm alive
Today I walk the streets of Albuquerque
Tomorrow somewhere else
Each day another scar, another story to tell
—◆—

You should see the sight that comes from my eyes
Nothing that should be exterminated escapes my eyes
I have one vision with many sharp fingers
I chew your world up and spit it out
Do you see me watch you bathe in filth?
Watch you choke on your dreams?
You should see the sight that comes from my eyes
—◆—

Today I crossed the Mississippi river
It was covered with ice and kept Illinois from moving
Grey cast iron sky driving snow falling dirty
Empty houses dip backed horses pigs graveyards baseball diamonds
A large building, the paint so worn away I could barely read
Smith and Wilson - Embalmers
The windows were broken out
The sun started going down
Darkness crept in slowly
It could have been Death taking a breather
—◆—

I've been to love
But you see I'm back here
At the end of the mission there's another waiting
I've been to the cardboard palaces of love and home
I turned them to ash
Now I'm back where things snap and bite
I want to be destroyed while on a mission
Not while wrapped in the cancerous embrace of love
Not trembling with shit running down my leg

In home's treacherous stable
That's why I'm right here
—◦—

Do you know them?
The little insult hurling embodiments of weakness
The ones who's voices resemble small dogs
The ones who run in circles
The ones who peck like the birds that pick shit off rhino's backs
Their words and gestures mean nothing
Without the strong they couldn't exist
Every once in awhile one of them gets crushed
Or better yet, back handed at a restaurant
A few drops of urine go down the leg
They get called a few names and get a different job
Spineless
—◦—

I can feel things breaking inside me
Show after show, night after night
It feels like glass in my guts
My head feels like I've been wringing out a washcloth
At the end I'm left in a desert
I don't know who I am
I lose big parts of myself out there
I do my best to get them back
I don't know if I pull it off
Or if I'm lying to myself
Or trying to make it real for lack of nothing better to do
At night I throw bricks at my soul
I cut myself on the splinters
And sit in quiet rooms trying to find myself again
It never ends
—◦—

It was an emotional overload for her
When I moved past her
I don't think her suicide helped her get over it
—◦—

I tell you
For me not to kill
Has become a total commitment to discipline
It would feel so good to torch this ugly place
—◦—

These mean ass ice covered streets

They hate everyone who has the bad luck
To have to walk on their faces
Sometimes they suck us into the cracks

When the truth hits your weak ass
It's going to break your goddamn skull
That's the way power treats force
You spineless little fuck
Get ready to crawl

I don't love you
I did for a few minutes but even then
It was just me loving myself with your body
I do that sometimes
So do you

The old man in the train station
Said that some of the bums were going to freeze solid tonight
He said that there was a war on
I know he's right

I will not compromise
My will is my savior
I can withstand any weather
If it doesn't kill me I will learn

It's war right now
Can you feel it in the air?
What, you can't?
You're dead

I try to get out of my body and into hers
It never works
Makes me feel unresolved and distant
Trapped inside my dick
I'm stupid

I want to be a snake
I want to find the ground with my guts
When I wrap myself around you baby
I gotcha

Let me use you
Let me inhabit you
Let me turn you to ash
—◁-

I wonder what happened to these people
He shouldn't have thrown that bottle at my head
Fuck'em and charge'em double next time
—◁-

I fucked this girl
Nice girl
Now I feel like I was alone the whole time
Like I stuck my dick into an empty house
Makes me want the real thing that much more
I want a woman that overwhelms me
One that commands my respect
—◁-

My thoughts turn into blades
I cut myself on myself
I work hard to protect myself from my self destructive nature
Sometimes I think that I only maintain myself
So I'll have something to kick very hard
My thoughts turn on my thoughts
I eat myself alive
I vomit myself into myself
I make myself sick
Sometimes I think that I could rupture all my blood cells
By thinking the wrong thing
It's a good thing I have a short attention span
It allows me to forget myself from time to time
—◁-

When I saw you the other night I wanted it to be different. I wanted to
go back to years ago. When I see you, part of me longs for that time.
When I see you now, I only feel a slight ache. I get mad at myself for
not feeling that overload that used to run through me. Perhaps part of
me has died or given up. Now you're just someone I know. When I see
you I look closely. I hope to see a spark of what it was that inspired such
heated unrest. There's part of it I can't let go. It's the third arm that
beats me. You're beautiful and you make me feel old and confused. I
don't know who I was. I only know who I am.
—◁-

Hating you makes me hate all the others
Hating you makes me hate the whole idea

It frees me so I can see you
Your attempts to infect me obviously didn't work
So you turned on yourself and called it something else
Like oppression
Or getting screwed by the powers that be
You make me laugh as I watch you sink
Finally meeting yourself and not recognizing the face
—◦

I sign my name to all my flights
All my break downs
All my calamities
I cannot disown them as others do
That would be like looking at your arm
And saying it wasn't yours
Because you didn't like the way it looked
I have no separation, no distance
I can register the destruction of thought
I know the alien and the enemy
I cannot turn it loose into the streets
And not recognize it as my own
I cannot abort myself
I cannot disown myself
I'm locked in here
If there was a key I never found it
If I did I would have thrown it away
—◦

No
I'm going to get away from you
I'm going to lock the door of my room and load my gun
I'm not going to blow my head off
I'm going to blow yours off if you try to come in
I'm going to sit until I go insane
All your talk and cheap noise
Is bringing me down to your level
I'm starting to feel like you
I can't do that to myself
I'm going for solitary refinement
You get me confused and wear me out
You and your emotional rescue
Don't reach out
I'm not there for you
I'm not that which you will hold onto until it finally dies

I am the frozen species
Go ahead, love me
You'll starve yourself to Death
There is some destruction going on tonight
It's all yours

The man telling the story about little kids blowing up in Vietnam
His anger fear fueled insanity doesn't escape me
The lines of eyeless wordless ones punished by existence
They don't escape my eyes
The vet who started to strangle me
As he went back to the jungle to bayonet babies
While we sat in the park
I can't take my eyes away
Sometimes I think I'm going to explode from what I see
It makes me want to tear my arms off and help
It makes me want to walk away
And never see another thing that breathes
Get a gun and wait for Death

You don't make me feel like you used to
That's why I'm leaving
That's why people leave each other
They come to their senses and get selfish again

I saw you last night
It's hard to believe I felt so strongly about you
I feel very old right now
Have you ever experienced something so great
That years later you regretted the whole thing
Seeing the hole it left in you?
I remembered how I used to lose sleep over you
When you made me hate everything
It was glorious
Now it's nothing
When we see each other we cover each other in dust
Some wars are over
Peace sickens me
I am an archaeologist searching through my own ruins
I can see the sun setting in your eyes
How dimly they shine through the dust

Restaurant Hell 1: The waitress is magic. She comes to the table and sticks her hand up her skirt. She gropes around for a moment and pulls out a plate with my omelet on it. She won't tell me how she does it. She won't tell me who her agent is. Not bad food though. I ask for a re-fill for my coffee and the cup goes straight up the skirt, she closes her eyes, makes a few choice grimaces and out it comes, hot and steaming. She's about to give it to me and she stops right before the cup reaches my hands. She looks at her crotch and then back at me and says "You want some milk in this?"

—◦—

Date Hell: We're making out in my car, nothing much you know just kissing. She says "Hey you wanna see something real cool?" And I figure what the hell you know? So she pulls down her drawers and she's got both, you know what I mean, both set ups. I'm not up-tight right, but this made me feel strange. She tells me to touch it. I ask her which one she wants me to touch. She looks at me and says that the choice is mine. Well I'm not a fag right, so I didn't want to be touching a dick, but at the same time I didn't want to be touching anything on this girl. Then it occurred to me that I didn't know if this was a chick with a dick or a dude with a puss, you know? I pretended that I was real tired and that I had to get some sleep to be ready for practice in the morning and then I split. It put some distance between us, but she's real nice, or he's real swell, hell I don't know.

—◦—

Gas Station Hell: My car was getting low on gas so I pulled into a gas station to fill up "Ninja" my souped up super beetle. I pull up to the regular pump and I'm about to get out and fill Ninja up when this attendant comes from out of nowhere and says "Welcome to Gas World, how may I be of service to you?" I tell him that I want 5 dollars of regular gas. He says "Ass gas or grass no one rides for free!" I say yea right and stare at the steering wheel. I look up a moment later and he's just standing there smiling at me. I ask him about the gas and he says "What, you say your mom has a big ass?" I tell him no I want some gas. He starts to sing. "Yes we got no bananas, no bananas today!" I ask him to put in the gas and leave out the jokes. He looks at me and asks what kind of gas I want, and I tell him 5 on regular will be fine. He says "Sassafras? What the hell are you talking about, this is a gas station not a space station. Are you on drugs?" I tell him that I'll get the gas myself And I start to get out of Ninja when he gives me an intense look and says " I wouldn't do that if I were you pal..." I back off and ask him about the gas again. He says "If you ask to touch my ass one more time I'll shoot you where you sit." I change my tack. I ask him if has any petrol. He says

"How did you know my name was Saul?" I looked behind me, there were no cars in this place. The guy's eyes were burning red. I fired up Ninja and we got the HELL out of there.

—◇—

Date Hell II: We where in my car making out, you know how it is. All at once she makes this grab for my dick. She looks at me real hard and says "I suck a mean dick, ask all your little fucking friends in class! Come on get hard right now! I'm going to suck the life right out of you!" I tell her that maybe we should wait until the movie starts at least. She punches me in the mouth, not real hard but hard enough to let me know that there was something on her mind. I was wiping the blood from my lip when she says "Oh look, you're bleeding, I'll help you." She starts sucking the blood from my lip and she starts making all these noises like she's some kind of damn pigeon. I get her off my face and tell her that I was going to get some popcorn. I get out of the car and get to the nearest phone I could find and call the cops. I know that it was probably the wrong thing to do but it seemed like the best thing at the time.

—◇—

Bus Hell: Let's see here, give this ol' canteen a shake, yep, there's a swallow or two left. It's been a long wait for the bus, been here a couple of days now. I don't mind, I called ahead to the doctor and told him that I would be a little late since I had to take the bus. What the hell...buzzards...get the HELL away from me. Yep, it's been a long wait for the #4 to Hollywood. The Doc said that I shouldn't wait too long with this here broken leg, he said that if I didn't get here soon enough he would have to re-break it and he said that would be 50 dollars extra. I'll tell you the truth, I don't have it. I might as well get back home and see what's on the tube, it's going to be a long walk with this crooked leg. It's always a long walk when you're in HELL.

—◇—

NY Penn Station Men's Room Hell: I got off the train with tears in my eyes. I didn't want to do it. I wanted to keep going, but as fate would have it I had to do business in the Evil Apple. The first thing that hit me was the smell, nothing smells like Penn Station. I went up the stairs and the first maniac came at me. I side stepped him and headed for the men's room. The place is packed, a bunch of guys with their dicks in their hands. I'm waiting my turn to step up and relieve myself. As luck would have it, all the fellows finished at once and the place all but emptied in seconds. I went over to the urinal. I saw behind me, a man staring. I thought to myself, what the hell would you want to be doing that for, there must be a better place to be than in an over heated poorly lit room inhaling the aroma of urine from all over the eastern seaboard.

It occurred to me that it might not be the best idea to have this guy behind me without being able to see him. I turn around and ask him as casually as possible what he is doing in the men's room with his back to the wall staring at me. He says nothing. I look down at my dick. Nothing is coming out of me. With all that is in me I am trying to coax the urine out of my body before the maniac gets it in his head that it's time to tear my head off. Finally with great will power, I managed to empty my bladder. I turned around to leave and he was still there smiling at me. I looked at his hand, he was holding a stop watch. I asked him if he got his kicks timing how long men urinated. He said that he did just that and asked me if I wanted to go out with him later. I said no thanks. His eyes turned red. It was Satan! I said "Oh Prince of Darkness, you are a kinky motherfucker!" he said "I maybe only the Prince of Darkness, but I am the King of Kink, now suck your ass out of here before I lock you in one of the stalls. Be gone!"

—◆

He was a hate machine
He told the woman as she was leaving him:
No one will ever understand you, all the do is try to destroy you. They want to kill you piece by piece. You won't know until it's too late. Your hate is the only thing you have to let you know that you're alive.
Fuck love
Look outside, where is the love
Go out into the world with your love
The streets will drink your blood
All you have at the end of the day is hate
He said that it wasn't protection
It was a bullshit detector
He said that they try to exchange your hate for fear
When you were empty of hate they could make you do what ever they wanted to, it's hate that keeps your eyes open. They will try to steal your eyes and fill them with their world, soon it's all you see.
I think he has a point
Love makes you weak, hate is the cure
I asked him about all the great works of art that were inspired by love
He said that he didn't think they were so great
He said that all the bullshit discussions couldn't change the way he felt
He said that hate make the world go round
People are afraid of what they really want
They make enemies of all the things that they would like to be
They condition themselves to not embrace what they are
Love is a clinging nausea

I tried to disagree with him
It was no use
I never saw a more honest look in anyone's eyes
—+

They write me from all over
One can't get women off his dick
Another can't get them to stay on
He wants to kill me
She wants to fuck me
They're having problems with their parents
They can talk to me a lot easier
At times it's hard to face
I let the mail sit for days
I can see the blood come from the envelopes
The sweat, fear and frustration
I don't know them but I do
It's past 5 in the morning now
I have been answering letters for 4 hours
That's me, Mr. Excitement on a Friday night
No time left to myself, I gave it all to these strangers
I could throw out all this mail
Hire someone to answer it politely
I could do that but I couldn't
I couldn't do that to someone who has been straight with me
I can't do that to the youth, besides
Everybody else does
—+

Nothing you do blows me away
I read your papers
15 year old boy found with 3 bullet holes in his head
You assholes torture each other every day
All your wars make perfect sense to me
Your acts of love are just acts
Kids dealing crack to kids
World War III so what
I don't hate you idiots for it, it's just the way you are
All your pain and suffering leaves me cold
This is not the time or place to be in need
Fuck all of you
—+

Let's do a song about the girl in college who fucked the frat boy and got
knocked up. The one who died screaming and convulsing in her room

from septic infection from the abortion.

About the kid from Nebraska who went to Vietnam and watched his guts cool on his legs before he died a virgin in the jungle.

About the girl who has been in a mental institution for 9 years and has been stuck with needles so many times she thinks she's a messenger from god to take the word's pain on her shoulders.

About the man on Death Row who has not seen a woman for 15 years.

About the boy who was made to fuck his mother while his father watched.

About the man who came home from work to find that his wife had cut their infant son in half and shot herself in the head.

About the mother who was too high on junk to see that her baby had fallen down the side of the bed and smothered to Death.

About the boy who is beaten regularly by his father and is afraid to tell anyone because he fears the fucker will kill him.

About the rich kid who fucked the girl, killed her and got away with it.

About the woman who threw her baby into a dumpster and when she heard the sound of the child's skull hitting the iron floor she ran away screaming and vomiting.

Let's sing

Touch me
Kick me
Make me crawl
Do something
Make me see that I'm alive
I need it bad
I feel dead
Stick something sharp into my flesh
Rip the lids off my eyes
Make me see
Torch me
My burning body will light up the night sky
It will make the Sun jealous

Black summer night
Incinerator breathing hard
Calling me down
I want it
Take me all the way

I have nothing else to want for
Except the chance to burn
I want a life time of summer nights
Seduce the sweat from my pores
Like a killer
Turn me on
Turn me up
Turn me loose

Shoot the boyfriend in the face
Pull her out of the front seat
Do lunch

She calls
It's ok if you don't want to have sex with me
But let's not throw the friendship away
I hung up on her
Friends?

It's getting dark out side but I can see clearly
The world around me is falling apart but I keep it together
The walls are closing in but I can still catch my breath
I can see my Death
I can see myself at the end, wearing out like a common fool
Right now I am the shadow man
I know that this will end
But right now I am the endless scar
I know that I will get old and easy to kill

Her eyes were always cold
By lying to myself
I could make believe they had some warmth
She was cold and wooden
I don't know why I stuck around
Maybe I was trying to prove how wrong a person could be
It's easy to cut yourself on your own edges

Beware the night
It has sharp teeth
It knows the ways of stealth
It carries a sharp blade
It cuts deep

The night has me in its spell
A shadow that follows me
Silent assassin
My reason for living
Come closer and let me see you
Before you kill me
I want to see myself in your eyes
—◦—

Nothing will happen to you
You will emerge from all this totally unscathed
They will not destroy you
All the things that you heard they do to others...
It's all a lie
Those things don't happen to real people
They only happen to those in the other world
They get hired by killers to get killed
You're safe from all storms
In case they get you mixed up about those people
Like the ones that die in plane crashes
They pay extra to have that happen
They didn't want to die alone
Imagine the woman that lives in the rooming house
One that slashed her wrists and left no note
You'll never have to do that
Your life will long endless bliss
Good night angel
—◦—

She's got cardboard tears
They fall from her face
She's got plastic emotions
She turns them on and off
She is energy efficient
She has glass eyes
She sees blindly, selectively
She has television instinct
I love to hear the sound she makes
When she short circuits herself
For a brief blinding instant she is real
—◦—

Don't push me
I've got a corner at my back
I've nowhere to go except over you
—◦—

That city is a wasteland
With all the cars whizzing by my eyes
With all the people moving up in the world
It's a wasteland
A gutted animal raped and devoured
A land of empty and filthy rooms
Your jaded dream is not a vision
The wasteland is not wonderful
It's a space pushed over by vicious children
Land of 1000 addictions
The endless suicide
You chainsmoke abortions
You drink dead water
You speak a dead language
You bought the whole thing
You don't even exist
—❖

It's raining in the desert tonight
I'm on the Southwest Chief going east
I'm looking at the black window
My face stares back
Good to be out of the room
Every once in awhile you get a break
I'm happy to be free and alone
—❖

4.20.88
Driving through Georgia
Shirt getting wet
Been moving south since noon
Saw the first palmetto an hour ago.
The sides of the road are flooded
The green is exploding
We nosedive south
Palm trees, pine trees
Last week I was in Boston
We pull for Tallahassee
Every road greets me
Like a black vein that runs through my marrow
After this is over I will be dead
But right now...
—❖

Georgia: Burnt down house. Fat white man, fat black man sitting on the front porch playing checkers. Sheriff at the gas station. Old woman in a rocking chair. Child playing in the dirt next to a trailer home. Old church. Man driving a tractor down the side of the road. Green trees, brown fields. Abandoned shack, swamp. Man burning garbage. Small lake with rowboat on shore. 3 men and a boy looking into the motor of a Model A. Sign for Cairo, GA. Central High Yellow Jackets football field. Stubborn unmoving sun. Thomasville train station. Endless two lane road cutting a path through impenetrable foliage. Days later: New Mexico. Flat rock plateaus. Red clay. Brush. Dry, hot, cloudless. Huge sky with black birds.

Her laughter grates against the air
She sounds like the end of 1000 nights of chain smoking
She's the dregs of a bad dream
Ex Junkie
She sucks me in and spits me out
She tells me about all the guys she's burned in the past
How she used them and the things they believed
She laughs and says: I'm a pro!
Lies fall from her mouth to the floor
They fall into the ashtray
Her perfume smells like Death and longing
Her eyes hunt and consume
They steal, they are the hungriest eyes I have ever seen
It's as if she's dying and she's sustained by what she sees
She hates men but she says that I'm different
She works her mouth across my waist
She looks up and tells me she knows what I like
Insane

Today is one of those days
Baton Rouge LA
The PA was late
The crew is building a stage out of wooden slats
We're in a roller rink in the middle of nowhere
I missed all the interviews I was supposed to do
There's no food to be found
It never ends
But then again

Are you dead
Are you alive

Are you in the middle
Do you feel anything at all
Does anything make you sweat
Does anything make you scream at night
Is there anything you want so bad
That you would get down on your knees and beg
They call me a freak
I am a flag pole that you can run up and down
I am something
Not someone
I make it easy for you
If I cut you would you bleed
Would you let me help you
I see you looking at me like you don't know me
I see you looking at me with disbelief
I hear your laughter roar past my ears
It's all over when I look into your eyes
That's where we know each other
All the lies fall to the ground
They become too heavy to pick up
That's where I leave you
—•

He learned about pain by studying the faces of others
He would go off by himself and try it
He didn't feel anything that made him want to stop
He couldn't feel pain
Everything felt good
He hired a guy to depress him
The guy got mad and left
He couldn't get our boy to stop laughing
One day he laughed so hard he choked and died smiling
—•

The ballad of no man
I am void
I am all things compacted into nothing
1000 ghetto sunrises see my incendiary eyes
Watch my burning footsteps
Don't get too close or I'll take you nowhere
I am all the empty rooms
Cheap light
Exhaled air
My heart is a lead bell ringing

My thoughts are pieces of broken glass
I'm getting out
I am that which can no longer be destroyed
I suck tears from the corpses of dreams
I am the emptiness
I sing the wordless tuneless dead song
This is my song
Listen to it rot

California highway at night, the last ditch for strangers
The two of them strapped in while the car burned
1978 Pinto wagon turned incinerator coffin
They just sat there taking it
The flames screamed against the sky
I watched the paint burn off the license plate
I've never seen anyone go like that
Up on the embankment the palms hissed laughter
Say good bye to the night
What a human way to go
All consuming fiery arms wrap yourselves around me tonight
Hold me
Burn the whole night through

This is your last chance to go nowhere
My car is up on blocks
Hop in, let's go

That woman I saw
I could write about her all night
Cruel mouth, scalpel eyes
She saw me looking at her
I thought she was going to spit on me
She carried beers to those idiots all night
She kissed that fucked up biker on her way out the door
She went to her car and split
I wish we were at her house right now, fucking

Alone looking for the quickest way to get to pain
I am my soul smasher love call Death trip
I slashed the wrists of Destiny and took total control
I watch the night strangle the sun
Hail night

Darkness, my brother

Fucking without kissing without talking
I bite your shoulder
You claw my back
Later you come out of the bathroom with a cigarette in your mouth
You say goodbye and I hear the engine of your car fade
I stare at the ceiling
Some might find that a bit shallow
Not you and I
We like it that way
We think that we have it beat by mutual denial
I like it when you're cold to me, it makes me respect you
If you ever showed me anything other than your animal need
I would never see you again
I don't want to know about your problems and your life
We are the real thing

Quick!
Like a gunshot!
Let's hide

He tells me he's doing better now
It's been a long upward crawl up from the sewer
The bottom floor was hell for real
He used to be addicted to junk
Now he's addicted to talking about
How he's not addicted to junk
Counting the days he's been clean
He talks about junk more now than when he was using it
Makes me think that no one gets away from it all the way
The more he talks, the more I see the monkey
Breathing down his neck
Singing sweetly in his ear
Telling him to come home
No one ever gets away
No one ever crawls all the way out
They become living documents
Tributes to the overwhelming claws of the 10 ton monkey

He stood on the roof
Threw a penny off and listened

A few seconds went by
Then he heard the faint bright sound of it hitting the cement
He looked up into the night sky
Clear, no planes, no clouds, nothing but darkness and stars
He threw another penny off and listened
He spat and listened to the barely audible splat
He threw himself off
All he heard was the wind

She asked me if I ever felt the desire to be held by a woman. I didn't say anything. She thought I was making up my mind and asked me again. I told her that I wasn't going to answer that. She said that she should keep her distance from me. She said that one morning I'll wake up one morning and find myself very alone. If we were on a cliff I think I would have pushed her off. There's nothing I hate more than people handing me lofty statements like they're these all knowing beings with supreme wisdom. Like they really know me, like they really know you. She doesn't know the war I come from. I said I had to leave, I would have rather spent the evening watching bugs die.

Come to my funeral
Sing me your dearest song
Climb into this funeral bed with me
Love this corpse
Play me your real music
It's alright
I won't tell anyone, I'm dead
I'll never betray you, I'm dead
Everything I say is final, get it?
Touch me, hold the corpse
It's cold I know
Fuck the memory, taste what was
I'm dead, hold me, make me miss life
Breathe into my mouth
Sleep with the dead
Look into my dead eyes, tell me the truth
Your one truth
I won't tell anyone
I'm dead
Where I'm going, no one cares to know
Touch this dead thing
Lie down with this rotting figure

Feel your thoughts melt
Your memories turn on you
Turn you into a self inflictor
Ride with the dead tonight
━━

I am Dead Man
I am un-numbered, un-filed
I am untouchable
I laugh at you everyday
Everything you do falls short of me
You can't kill me, I'm Dead Man
I threw myself away before you could get to me with your disease
You fucking cripples
I am the great failure
The endless botched suicide attempt
The super charged embarrassment
I am all the things that fell short
I am all disappointment
I manufacture all the things that you hate in yourself
I am all your secrets
You'll never get to me
I'll be the hot monkey on your back for the rest of your life
I am king of the modern day car crash
I am the ten-ton alienator machine
I inject hope into you like a disease
I drain it from you to cause you pain
I make you cause yourself pain
That's the way it should be
You're always eager to blame others for your discontent
I like to run you up against yourself
Watch you drown in self pity
I breathe on you so hard you back wants to break
When I kiss you, you're gone forever
You hate me?
No
You don't deserve to hate me
You have to learn to hate yourself better
I'm here to help you until Death motherfucker
━━

There's not much to life
Boom boom
There's not much to life

Boom bang
She's got a grey room
It feels like a tomb
She feels dead all the time
At the job, on the street, everywhere
There's not much to life
She doesn't feel it when he fucks her
He pays no attention
She looks at the ceiling while he grunts
He's thinking of someone he saw in a movie
There's not much to life
She's always alone, no matter who she's with
Men that stare at her tits when she serves their food
Can't make her feel, can't make her care
One will ask her what her name is
She says: Look at the name tag sir
She hears the word bitch as she walks away
4 hour shift, 10 hour shift, it all feels the same
When she gets home she calls no one, leaves the lights off
Waits for sleep or Death
When you're lucky you get pain
When you're not you get nothing
There's not much to life

Not much light in my dead room tonight
The walls are killing me
The night is poisoning me
Slow and silent
Like sliding down the throat of something huge
The room waits for me to die
The room has all the time it wants
The room is eternity
The room has killed many before me
Drove them insane and sent them to hell
The room controls the environment
The love song killer
The soul smasher
To the dead room I conform

You see what they do when they get the chance
They rape and kill and steal
Can you feel their disease?

Do you ever feel like a prisoner?
Like you're being sucked dry?
Do you ever feel hated?
Do you ever feel you're destroyed by them everyday?
They are not your friends
━╋

4 Wall Blues
Walking home to a hot room tonight
No one will be there except me
My eyes saw too much dirt today
Been walking a long time
Silence waits for me
I have a hard time with depression
The beast that follows me
Makes me say things I don't want to
Tonight I'm walking with the Beast
Onward to the soul drain
One more shackle, one more nail
I close my eyes and see a dark cloud
I don't want to feel like this
I feel the big teeth biting down
They got me in their grip
I'm going down low and hard tonight
The street lights pass overhead
The cars pass, some of them yell at me
I breathe their exhaust and keep walking
You can't let people get too close to you
It never works out
The closer they get the more they'll hurt you
They can't help themselves
The room is all around me
It had all the bad trips laid out and ready
Filling me with poison
I heard one wall say to another
Let's get him good tonight
   The wall starts in: You're not as good as you used to be, I think you're
trying extra hard to cover the fact that you lost it. Face it, you can fool
them but you can't fool us. You're a walking joke.
   I heard another wall chime in: A lot of people talk shit about you
when you're not around. You know why? Because you suck. All you do
is fill rooms with the sound of your voice, you go all over the place ad
all you do is talk. You're insecure, it's the biggest thing you have going

for you. Women laugh in your face because they see a child looking back at them. The only reason you have a ton of shit to deal with is because you have so much of it in you.

All the walls started laughing

After a while one said: Maybe you should just kill yourself. You'll never get what you want. What do you want, the same things that you always want that you never get. Why don't you give up and call it quits. Get the gun out of the drawer and go for it you weak slob. Do something right for a change.

One of the other walls got mad and said: Don't tell him to kill himself, then we won't have him around to fuck with. Hey, you know you're a surface level piece of shit, you only think of yourself no matter what you say. Oh forget it, you're not worth my time.

Another wall spoke up: You live in a lie, you bury yourself in work so you won't have to deal with the fact that you were a lot better years ago. Why don't you wake up and smell the coffee. The truth is something you can't face. The truth scares the shit out of you.

It's hard to keep shit together
Depression is always there, waiting to hammer down
Makes it hard to be around others for any sustained period of time
When I extend myself to others I always regret it
At the end of it I always feel I said too much
I get mad when I feel the need to communicate with them
They ask questions like tourists walking around my face
It's a constant battle to hold back the anger and the rage
Sometimes when I see them I want to kill them all
Some of the things they have done to me over the years
Burned me with cigarettes and were allowed to walk away
Seems to me that you should get killed for doing shit like that
I know this and that's what keeps me separated from them all the time
I know I'm a freak
They don't like it when they see themselves in me
It makes them violent and makes me stronger

Streets full of eyes checking me out
I listen to the report
The black guys on the basketball court think I'm hot
They laugh and cheer as I pass
Like I really need this shit
I feel like I got the wrong planet
When I try to be close to someone

I temporarily forget that they are one of them
Rooms full of eyes
Always looking
I don't like them like I used to
They don't get to me like they used to either
They used to get me all wound up
Then one day I realized that it's all nothing
Now I see them differently
I see right through them
I don't hear them the same way either
They sound like little dogs yapping
It doesn't count
It doesn't matter
It doesn't exist
—◦

I see them yes I see them
Like pale hairless cattle
Packed into subway cars rushing off to the circus
They all want to get in the center ring
Sick and scared I see them running
They sweat when they're cold, cold blooded
You would think they would have a little more imagination
I have no desire to die like my father and mother died
They way they died thousands of times
Corralled, fed shit, made to stand in line
Sent on errands and degraded by clowns
I don't want to go up on any of the crosses
I'm tired of hearing about the crosses
The tired, empty, tiny pain
Don't try to make it matter to me
Have you ever seen a man running to catch a bus
An overweight man running like he's going to die
Could you imagine how that would hurt
Your heart pounding
Sweating for the boss
Eyes bugging out
They got tricked a long time ago
Tell me it's not that way for you too
Don't tell me that they made you hard and steely eyed
Jaded and short of breath
You have to be careful
They're everywhere
—◦

Those who know are the lucky ones
The ones that don't look lucky really are
It's the ones that know they're sick that stand a chance
They know there's a war on
The world is a bad place that kills people
The strong are killed along with the weak
The weak take longer, they hide in the cracks
It's easy to see the sick ones
The ones choking on life
Trying to choke the life out of life
Battling the elements
You see the cowards and their doctrine of cowardice
They peer timidly from their tombs
They feel convenient pain
Something for a thrill
The strong live
The weak take years to die
My heart goes to the ones that struggle
The ones that search and destroy
More savagery, more beauty, more life

I keep telling myself that I'm not bitter
That their poison has not gotten to me
That I have risen above their petty timid reality
That they have not mutilated my mind
That I have not been broken and made to crawl
I am filled with burning rage
I feel it rise inside me and it makes me choke
I think back to the past
I see that I was taken for a ride by them
Friends, parents
My father calling me "mister"
I spend a lot of time spitting out pieces of myself
Pieces that have been ripped and torn
Ridding their blood from my blood
Wondering who I am underneath the scar tissue
After all this, what will be left
Will I be able to recognize myself
Will I know what to do?

I'm not a bolt of lightning scarring the night sky
I'm not a genius

But even I can see what's in store
They'll try to shove you down your own throat
They'll make you hate your guts
Don't live on excuses
They will kill you
The good times aren't here
They'll tell you otherwise
My pain and hate are what save me
Hope came to my house
I shot it on the front porch
It bled wine cooler

I see your face in my mind and I pull away from myself
It's like I'm spitting on my soul
I cause myself pain by thinking of you
I think of you and it's the worst
Usually people don't mean that much to me
You're different
I think of you and I fall into a hole
I see your eyes in other women
It makes me small and foolish
This has no punch line
It's just a locked groove
I miss you

The room is my helper tonight
The walls stare me down
I turn on myself, can't stop turning
The room is a womb that kills
Makes me an expert in the making of high grade depression
I'm tired of talk
The sound of their voices makes me want to scream
Maybe I can sit in this room until I die
That would be so good, so gutless, so fitting
I would know myself so well by then
I wouldn't have to think

This place fills me with hate
They try to tell me about love
I can't see it on this road
Screaming about love as they run forward with knives
I had to get rid of love to survive

Love was trying to kill me so I learned hate
They can't stop the fire that burns inside me
They can't stop the hate machine
You tell me that love is the answer
Has it ever occurred to you
How fucked up you are?
They took your identity
The rest came only too easily
You crumble
All your books will not help you now
I can't wait for a lot of years to pass
I want to be the one to see you and your sad face
As you drag it to the Death you fear so much
And do so much to hurry forward
—

Tonight depression beats down on me with lead hands
The night holds me prisoner
Inside my brain I smolder with violence
I'm on a slow burn that's turning me to ash
I don't sing love songs
There's too many holes shot through them
I don't feel lonely
For who, for what?
They'll sell you out in a minute
Hate is the only thing that lasts
Hate is always at the bottom of the cup
You see hope running out of the house
With blood streaming from its asshole
You see hate standing on the front porch
Laughing, zipping up its pants
Love lies and never pays the rent
Neither does hate but it never makes you think it will
So I'm here tonight, unmoved
—

I know what I'm doing
I'm killing myself slowly
It's an addiction to destruction
These places I go, these Death houses
Endless highways to Death
All roads going to Death
All the time rattling my bones
Dying over and over

Looking for the big rise
It's one big scream
The big night
The huge overwhelming dark
Sucking the air out of my lungs
Scorching my dreams
Driving down a dark throat
It's nothing but a Death trip

Sometimes the only thing that sees me through is hate
It make me see clearly
Love makes me blind
I always regret love
I have never regretted hate
In the middle of nowhere with all against me
I use hate to endure
I like hate better than sex
It makes me burn brightly
Hate makes me think I'm a genius
It's like an aspirin for my soul
No money, strangers in my face
Good thing I have hate
Hate keeps my stitches from ripping apart
Sometimes it feels good to be alive
The rest of the time it's a joke

Budapest
Night time
You and I standing against a wall
We are burning
Your breath on my neck
Your nails in my shoulders
Our bodies locked and grinding
Your boyfriend in the apartment
Drinking vodka, listening to rock and roll
He knows that we're gone and I bet he doesn't care too much
There's not a lot he can do about it
I've been on both sides of this one

Nietzsche said it best
He called them Tiny Masters
Even though you could break my jaw

I still believe your fist is small
You got so much nothing
It looks like something to many
But not to me
So many of you
Kings of cheap talk
Your eyes sweat in their sockets
Small thoughts, small dreams
You don't destroy
You just wear things down
Tiny Masters
Life's parasites
Strong ideas in your weak mind
Send you staggering to your corner
You cover the cities in shit
The future really does belong to you

PASSING THROUGH

-The factories torture the evening skies of Coventry
-The filthy grinning wino clutches a large bottle of wine and staggers into an alley in Leeds
-The placard outside the church says "No god, no hope. Know god, know hope." I think to myself: Know hope, know disease.
-A woman passes me, her perfume is the same as the shit my step-mother wore. It makes my stomach turn.
-I look into the window of the house where I wrote all the songs for Hot Animal Machine. It has a for rent sign up. The table is in the same place, the same postcards are tacked to the wall.
-A bum blocks the sidewalk, he wants money for a cup of tea, his breath reeks of liquor.
-The flight attendants make jokes about the large breasted passenger.
-The factories are full of square eyed windows. I see smoke, flames and steam. I smell the stench. I think to myself that someone will be working in there for 15 years without quitting.
-A car load of gay boys pull up next to me as I walk and ask me if I want to go for a ride.
-A man and a woman search a dumpster for food, they pull out rotting vegetables. A van pulls up, a man with a suit gets out. His suit makes him seem impervious to the fate of the garbage eaters.
-I sit in a public park and look at the teenagers smoking like there's no tomorrow. They look over at me and I start laughing in their faces.
-A beautiful woman gets out of the driver's side of a Jaguar. A fat little

man gets out the other side. I wish she would drop him and take me with her. I'm waiting for the bus with a 12 oz from 7-11, I am dirty and crazy looking. She eyes me with disgust and walks away with the worm man. He looks back at me and smiles.

—⋆

She left me last night
The sun came up this morning
It looked great

—⋆

I got hit with a stone that was thrown
Through the wire of a long distance telephone
Static on the line couldn't get through
She told me she didn't want to see me anymore
Not me anymore
Then she hung up
I sat down on the bed of 100 hotel rooms
Everything got hollow and back to normal
I guess I'm free to go out and make other mistakes

—⋆

Child of the fist
Here lies the lie of experience
Hard heat and heavy step
Aware, ready to wince recoil and attack
Constantly in the corner
On the ropes
If you were thinking about it I wouldn't do it
His hostility is handed down
He was stepped on and nearly destroyed
The eyes give him away every time
You can see the animal rising
Child of the fist
Lord of the solitary refinement
The ear mark of destructive genius
Genius through brutality and fear
A man in touch with the ultimate perception
Instinct

—⋆

A bullet could touch me
Make me feel the way I do now
She came and left and came and then left for good
I feel mean and torn up
I'm not a push me pull you

Well I guess I am
Look at me with the floor filling my eyes
The painful forest
The woman I touch
I crawl away and try to heal
It's bad and the lights are dim
It smells like a circus tonight
—◦

Bait for the sharks that wait in the dark
Ready to jump out shake your hand and make you a deal
A human deal
Make you into a dinner talk show host
And then they turn you into scrap metal
Don't let them take the air out of your tits
—◦

In the middle of Silverlake I live in a square room
The street light shining down
Make all the broken safety glass
From the cars that got broken into
Shine like crime lit diamonds
—◦

The filth
The pool of dried vomit at the bus stop
The jeering youths in the passing car
The man getting busted by the pigs
Scar maker
Big cement fist to kiss
Alienator
Disease spreader
Bruises into my flesh
Welts rising in this bad exhaust dream
In this pummeling madness
It gets easier to die and fail
Your feet find themselves in line
My cancer heart!
It was always like this
Pull back the scar curtain
Roll back the iron lining
You'll find someone who remembers other times
But one who also crouches and waits
For the cheap bite of the weak
Who live and sneak peeks

At the strong who aren't long for the suicide song
Amen, good night, come here, I won't hurt you
Yes I know it's bad
But you get good at lying to yourself
—◁–

Something
Someone
Some power, force, unrestrained act of will
Take me out of here
I want to feel myself in your grip
If you're going to crush me go ahead
I can't find anything to live for
I'm not interested in their trophies
They're turning all the songs
Into tarnished coppers at the bottom of a tin cup
So smash me
Reality
Big soul incinerator
So run me
Road
Big time stomper
I want blood
I want a 10 star storm
Blow me into the next time zone
I'll see you next time
In the next crime
I'll burn and freeze alone
But don't leave me here
To eat dust and drink lie filled water
I don't want the shallow mind grave
I need something deep
Take me and destroy me
But don't leave me in this
—◁–

The mission
The burning idea
Blinds me to obstacles, numbs me to pain
Turns me mute makes them into strangers
I know the flesh is weak
It falls away
So easily swept and cleared
There's one thing that can carry us through

The idea
The idea makes us strong
Embrace the power
The world is full of creeps
Watch them crawl
Don't get too close
They'll pull you down
Keep the idea intact
Get to that power
I'm not talking about money
I'm talking about power, the idea
You'll never have to crawl
You'll never have to be one of them
If you keep the idea, embrace the power
I know that skin is only skin deep
Look past it
Don't fool yourself
Don't go insane
Get to the power

What do I have to do to get to you
What do I have to go through to get close to you
Your voice, your eyes
You make sense
You touch me and I'm alive
Show me the jungle
I'll level it
Show me the village
I'll incinerate it
It's pure this animal need
It's real life's endless greed
Consuming, burning
Night by night I'm strung together
Night by night I'm torn apart
Where are you, everything's burning
Where are you, I'm being destroyed
Hurry hurry
Over over

Walk with fire
Walk alone
This life has lost it's shiny appeal

I'm not young and I'm looking at the end
I'm terminal
A lifer
I'm taking this one to the end of the line

2 AM bus ride
Heading east on Hollywood
The dead men are riding tonight
Going to Crenshaw, downtown, Lawndale, Long Beach, Echo Park
It's all the same, a shit pit
The lucky ones are getting off work
They get on like hollow numbers
The occasional wave of recognition
Drinking beers in paper bags
A hard ride to the bottom

Hater hater incinerator
Boiling human torch turning the streets into rivers
Watching the drowning rats race to the bottom
I am a public servant
Pest exterminator
I work for the roaches...
They want to get rid of you
Hideous imperfections, lie livers
It's a miracle you survive
The time of your miracle will soon be over
A new one will arise
Reality will rear its ugly head
All I'm doing is rolling out the red carpet
Together we will put the balance back
I'm a public servant
I'll be there to clean up the waste
You're all filthy children
All your toys are broken now
It's high time

I feel Death in the hot night
I can taste it as it breathes down on me
I hear it in every sound
I want you to come down here with me in the hot night
I want you to lay your mortality down on mine
We're dying all the time

Can't you feel it?
I want to taste your Death trip
Let's kill time
They never do you know
They don't do a damn thing to time
Time mocks their every step
Time begs for confrontation but rarely gets a run for its money
Time hates me
I have time by the throat and I'm squeezing it for all it's worth
I stalk time through uncertain shadows
I'm a time killer
—

My beautiful animal lover
Dawn quickly approaches with its dull grey film
Painting the street with its weak light
I'm disappearing as I write this
I cannot sing to you my savage songs of war and desire
Until night beats its thunder drum again
Good bye until the absence of light takes the blinders from our eyes
—

I'm in my room sitting still
I just returned from the jungle
Many nights of deafening storms have passed through me
Now I sit and they're all coming back at once
The roar is tearing me up
Makes me want to break things
I know what I am
I'm one of the only ones left
I surround myself with myself
I wrap myself with the roar of the storm
I say nothing to them
I am the only one in my world
Through the destruction nights I crawl
I turn them away from me
I shove the shining pillar down their throats
I leave them to themselves
They don't get close
Their world is weak
Their words are bad jokes that litter my ears
I find comfort in the One
I learned there was no back-up anywhere else
—

The scars of inspiration
Last year when I was with you
You filled my life with lost hours
Many Deaths filled my room thinking of you
Hot nights spent with you left scars on my soul
You spat me out
For a long time there was pain and strife in my brain
Thinking of you made me want to rip myself to shreds
I did so
You should have seen me
It was beautiful
I unleashed myself on myself
I lost and won and scarred myself perfectly
And then like a curse
Your memory stopped tormenting me
I tried to bring it back from the dead
So I could beat myself with it
It was no use, I had used you up
I searched for other women
To inspire me to destruction
I found them but they weren't as good as you
They only went so far
They never made me feel totally powerless
You lied better
You made me hate myself more than any of the others
You were the best
The other day I got a letter from you
You said that had been thinking of me
And how bad you felt about leaving me in the ghetto
You said you wanted to see me again
The months have been so dead
I can't wait to see you again
I want better lies, better sex
You have to make me want you so bad
That when you leave me again
I'll unleash a storm on myself and disappear
I know you can do it
I need
Inspiration
—❦—

Through the black jungle night I called you
The heat and dark were strangling me

Turning me on myself
My entire body, every pore screaming out for you
Pure raw animal sound
Sweat burned my skin
Night after night
I want to taste you right now
I want to smell your sweat right now
I want to hear you scream
I want to feel your teeth dig into me
I want you to destroy me
I want you, do you hear me?
Do you hear me screaming through the blackness?
I'm coming for you
I'm not taking no for an answer
I know you want me

We started with pain
It got worse
The pain became our reason for being together
I couldn't take it any more
I was awoken by the sound of my heart beating hollow
I was bloodless and numb
I gave you all the pain that I could muster
Corpse-like I stumbled from your room to the alien world
In search of new pain

Watch out for the clowns
They will lie in your face
And play games with your good nature
They will leave you empty of blood
As they laugh and run down the road
To the next game
Don't lose yourself in their cheap war
It's easy to tell a clown
Watch the eyes when you ask a direct question
When the answer isn't an answer you know for sure
Pushy cons, little clowns with cheap weapons
Why are the weak permitted to live
Because you can get put behind bars for the rest of your life
For putting garbage in its place

I'm back from another tour

I'm sitting in my room dealing with the silence
I'm harder than when I left last time
Coal turning into diamonds
Talking to less people
Taking the phone off the hook for days
The more I'm around them
The less I want to have anything to do with them
They scar me, they leave me wracked and empty
I know all their moves
I know what they're going to say before they do
It's a process, turning inward, folding and folding
Compressing, coal into diamond
At this point I'm the only that I'm close to
The only one I want to know
I'm tired of putting myself in front of their eyes
And seeing nothing come back
How long did they think I was going to do that for?
I'm leaving for my jungle, my gleaming Over World
I can't get close to you
I reached out for you and got myself instead
Here I am

When I sleep I have dreams
Hands around my throat
Thousands of hands around my throat
Take me to the Over World
Take me into the bright night
Take me into the gleaming jungle

The hate that burns inside me
The hate they can't stop
The hate I can't diffuse
I can't tell you anything about it
Words don't work
So we just shut up and fuck

Year after year your cities continue to destroy themselves
I watch them stab themselves, use dirty needles
Cities chew you up with iron teeth
Nowhere men, nowhere women
You whore yourselves daily
You can never kill yourselves enough

Always looking to get the latest disease
I spit on your heads
You're turning people like me into heroes

There are only a few of us left
The weak seek to destroy us
I'm tough and keen eyed
My sense of smell is sharp
I would think nothing of wasting one them
They would try to do the same to me
There's little time left
There's only a few of us out there

Terms of Derangement parts 1-5
1: I think you're full of shit
I think you like the sound of your voice
Why are you so fake
I don't know what you want
It sure as hell isn't me
How can you expect me to get close to you
When you walk away and hide behind your eyes?
I think you're standing in front of a door
Guarding it to make me want in
It's a glass door I can see through
The room is empty
Your words are hollow, your eyes are beautiful
I like how they used to shine
Now I see that it was I who made them shine
You had nothing
You use people, they adore you
While they bleed to Death at your feet
I'm tired of trying to love a cardboard box

2: I could destroy myself over you
Rip myself to shreds and lie mangled at your feet
And I would
If I thought it would mean anything to you
If I thought you would do anything more
Than just step over me
And change the channel

3: I went to her and asked

What she wanted from me
She was silent
I asked her if she wanted me
She said nothing
I asked her politely
What the fuck her deal was
She just stared at me

4: I remember this shit from the last time I was with you
I know you enough to know that there's not much to you
My scars have brains
They have memories
I've grown smarter and harder
Sometimes I look to get cut
Because the healing teaches me so much
The last time I was with you
So many incisions
Now, I wrap your hair around my fingers
And over my scars
I wrap your lies around me

5: You're a joke and I'm laughing
I would like the chance to respect you
But I'll just use you instead
You don't know the difference

Never again will I tell you anything about myself. You will hear things come out of my mouth but they will be lies and diversions. I'm doing an experiment with you. I always told you the truth and all I got back was lies. Now I'll lie to you and see what happens. I'm tired of feeling like shit for having opened up to you, from now on I'm going to imitate you and see what happens. I'm going to act dull and simple, just like you.

For so long I resisted, I told myself that I was wrong about you. A long time ago my hatred spoke to me in clear simple words. I saw things for what they were and it filled me with hate. To see things as they are is to hate. For a while I tried to fit into their world of love and blindness and found it to be violent and filthy. I was filled with dirt after listening to their words of lies and desperation. I became part of their losing world. I can't see how they take it year after year. Perhaps they're so numb that they don't even feel it. This morning my hatred came to me and filled with light and clarity. I want to drop a bomb on this shit. I think at this point it's the best thing I can do. My hate burns clean.

—◆—

Dream for the future night
I walk your streets
My breath is filled with the stench of garbage
You might as well shit on yourselves
You wait for the other pigs to hose you off
When I walk your streets I think of bombs
I want to see the whole shit house go up in flames
It would be good to see you burn
Burn all the way to ash
It would be good to see you do something all the way
I should line you up and shoot you in the street
Right in front of your fucked up apartment building
You could fall right in with the other pieces of garbage
I am right about this
I live to destroy your world
I'm the best thing that ever happened to you

—◆—

The Rhythm of Decline
Your world is crumbling
Falling apart in front of your eyes
All things beating in the Rhythm of Decline
Soon it will all be over
You'll wonder why as you get shoved into the train
Smell the garbage
Shake your own hand
Now bite it
Congratulations
You're a success
I am the Sanitation Engineer
You can call me Almighty

—◆—

You can't take the truth
It scares you
Makes you shoot guns
You can't stand reality
You create plastic heavens everywhere you can
Desperately try to vacation while it all rots
The truth follows you with hot breath
It will bring you to your knees

—◆—

The truth will destroy all the people that I hate

Overworld Jollies
Another day has been torn away from my grasp
In the stillness of this cancerous night
I write to you from a place on high
The Overworld
Safe from your bullets and disease
All day I walked through the streets
I endured your poison
The Rhythm of Death
The Rhythm of Decline
Bang
A pig's dick slides into another pig's mouth
This is the way you do things
I rode the bus
I watched the boys sell their dicks on the Blvd
You and yours are on the way out
Dead music
The dead fucking the dead
Clapping for each other
Your endless fuck
Your endless funeral march
Sadomasochistic rituals, like breathing
I can see right through you
Attend to your jails you pricks
Here I come
I'm here to clean
To you I am a god
I can help you
Pass the needle
Pass the gun
Pass the ozone
You rape what you sow
Do you think if they executed prisoners
On pay-per-view
You think it would make a lot of money?
You should get one of your pig friends on that right away
My thunder never stops roaring
There will be no end to this storm
You made the mess
And now you're going to be the victims of it

You have a word for things you can't handle
Negative
You've been dragging the Truth's face in the filth
But now you'll choke
My hatred is the only clean thing in your world
—◦—

You and me
Why do we lie to each other so much
Maybe it's the only thing we have between us
When we're together I keep wondering
Which one of will start laughing first
At how full of shit we are
Neither of us puts down the script
We keep dancing in a locked groove
One day we're going to wake up and find ourselves very alone
I don't think we should worry about it
We'll find a way to get out of it
We've come this far
—◦—

When we're together we play tapes
You put in yours and I put in mine
We press play
We have a relationship
Isn't it pathetic that we can fuck
But can't look each other in the eyes?
—◦—

From hell to hell on a rope I swing
So many sets of eyes before I pass
Night after night rips across my flesh
Confession after confession
I feel rung out at the end of each one
I manage to find new parts of myself to destroy
Memories come like assassins
I want to smash all mirrors
Enough reflection
When I think too much
I stab myself in the back
I must move forward
I look for the rope to swing to the next hot place
It's getting harder to see the explosions
They are moving in, castrating the thunder
Turning it all into wall paper

They kill my nights
Memories get me when I'm weak
I Must break out of this room

—

There's a small part of my heart that's always sad
Part of me that walks with a slow aching step
Forever longing
The beauty of that
To be forever longing
Too much joy makes the time pass too quickly
A bit of sadness slows things down so you can see it
Makes the sun set slower
The poison of joy
They cannot imagine a beauty in sadness
They stay away
They never get past the surface
When I fall down inside I find new parts
It's like digging for soul's gold
I never want to become a stranger to the downside
That which moves me when I cannot be moved
The great longing, the great sadness
That's my inspiration
Filling the void
Filling the grave
Filling out the time card

—

I told her so much tonight
I told her of the great longing
The endlessness that I feel
I told her the things that mattered to me
And how hard it is to find things that matter
I thought I was making a lot of sense
When I saw the cold door of her eyes
I stopped talking and went back to my jungle
I feel homeless in their eyes
Surrounded by a wasteland in their embrace
Their everywhere is my nowhere
I'm tired of feeling lost and empty in their oasis
Life is not too short

—

Once they get in they never seem to get out again
They get trapped like roaches in a roach hotel

[Handwritten annotations:] Sadness madness / hot & cold spells / The ~~depression~~ Alcoholic / melting away to forget / your pain / Destroying me & making me / insane / ~~emotions hr~~ / Never get solved in / this never ending / stage / your face, your stench / Equals my rage

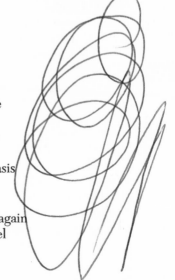

The big house of love
A big run down house that never sleeps
Life waits outside
I see the few crawling survivors
On their hands and knees going out the back door
Cut and bleeding they curl up and die
Some of the fools try to get back in
They try to break in the side window
They get their ass kicked and swear it's the best
It looks like a torture chamber
I don't play that shit
They can call me anything they want
I always see through
I always look at them as they crawl
They're lost in love
I'm lost in something else

I don't know when it happened
Parts of me died
I don't know if they all died at once
Or if it was in installments
Maybe I killed them off
Too many nights trying to destroy my weakness
In front of strangers
Maybe I did it in hotel rooms dotted all over
When I look into your eyes
I don't feel the way I used to
It's not you, you're beautiful as always
It's me, I'm dying piece by piece
Things don't seem as good as they used to
Maybe I'm growing old
Remember when someone's touch
Could send you to another world?
When it was the only thing you needed?
I feel like a soldier finishing the mission
I don't know if I'm a as stupid as I used to be
Half of life is fucking up
The other half is dealing with it
If I had tears
They would be hollow

Some nights I try not to think too much

Loneliness creeps into my thoughts
I see how alone I am
On the good nights I'm distracted
On the other nights it's all there is
That's why I keep busy all the time
I make things to do to take up the time
The more I do the more I see the emptiness
On a lonely axis I turn
Sometimes I want to paint all the windows black
Somehow thinking that it will all go away
It's hard to be here

 # 1

Keep walking these battered streets
Scared and sullen streets
They gotcha
You try to stay clean of the full on disease
But they gotcha
They run the game
They're in charge of all that good looking shit
This city turns people into losers
There's no escape, no outlet
People hacking off parts of their souls
They give readily to the great castrator
As time passes
The machine gets more refined
Easier to get to
More deadly
A world of whoredom

Take me into your heart
Swallow me whole
All the way down
Let me run wild in your dreams
Let me go and tear through you
Let me see what you're made of from the inside
Let me take hold
Let me wrap my hand around your soul
Only for a little while
A life time isn't all that long
You can't keep me out
You thought you had a choice
You thought you had a thought of your own

I think I'll destroy you and waste you time
I'll make you think I'm all there is to life
I use you up as you go down the line
I
Am
Lust
⊶

The streets by my house are covered with garbage
Every few blocks there's a pile of safety glass
Someone got their car broken into
The city chokes on black blood and old needles
Cheap gasoline and red wine
We get the drugs flown in
We kill ourselves exotically
Outside the bars in my neighborhood
There's sometimes blood on the sidewalk
Someone got stabbed down the street recently
Made the Times
The side walks make hollow sounds when I walk
I know it's ready to cave in
I don't want to forget
One scream, one gunshot
I want to remember it all
The place I'm going doesn't have time for decadence
My television has no channels
You can't touch me
You can't sell me anything
⊶

Death
I will stay with you until the end
I will walk this fire trail with you
Until one of us is destroyed
I will guard you in your sleep
Your dreams will be worry free
You will be safe with me
I know I'm safe with you
I trust you
I hear them talk
They don't make sense like you do
When you talk I listen
When you touch me
I feel it

Nothing will take me from you
I am joined with you
—❖

I thought that after her
There would be nothing
Shows you how wrong you can be
—❖

You tell me to come close
When I do you tell me to get away
Some may think you're hard to figure out
I have you figured out
You're full of shit
You have blue eyes and a hollow heart
Words fall out of your mouth
Like someone pulled a string out of your back
You're like a video game
—❖

She kept telling me about how she had been going to the clinic and
staying clean. It's all she talked about. She said that she had to stay away
from all of her friends that were still doing it. They should hand out
manuals with dime bags telling you how to creatively lie to your straight
friends and make them think that you're clean so they'll hang out with
you and let you into their houses even after you ripped them off a
couple of times. I hear the same shit from junkies, they're always so in
control. She came stumbling out of my bathroom high as shit. She
passed out on my couch and didn't get up until the next morning. She
told me she was straight even when I gave her back the cap to the
syringe she had left in the sink. As I was kicking her out of my house she
asked me what she was going to do. I gave her bus fare and told her that
I had no idea. Junkies always seem to come up with something don't
they? There's no such thing as an ex-junkie. No one ever gets away.
—❖

I feel good like a loaded gun feels good
Like an electric chair feels good
Headed out for the great light
—❖

The maggots boiling in the can of meat
They tell me about what happens
To things that are set out to rot
Why do I smell smoke in my dreams
They'll kill you with your own secrets
Anger boiling in the American ghettos

Nothing will come soon enough
Nothing will make enough sense
Nothing will be strong enough
Nothing will be there to wipe the slate clean
Open up my head and find this
—

Where I live is filthy
Even the cement is rotting
I pass the hotel
There's a woman sitting out front
Her knees are scabby and she looks like shit
She sees me and gets up to hit me for change
I sidestep and keep moving
I will not help the disease
I pass the spray painted walls
Barb wire, razor wire, vacant lots
Los Angeles is rotting
I see a palm tree with a poster tacked to it
"Stand Proud!"
Sure, but don't get any dogshit on you
Don't be late
Don't get shot
Don't be here after dark
—

You thought that they were your friends
You're on the ground and sinking
You see that you were wrong
No one will pick you up
That's what they do best
They let you fall
They tell you that you're beautiful
Can't you see what they've done to you
They wrecked your beautiful face
They sold your smile
They turned you into garbage
You fell hard
I came running
It was too late
They stole the jewels from your eyes
The last time I saw you
You were a museum piece
A history lesson

A walking book on how to be ugly
Who to stay away from
It's too late for you
Hollywood kills another
Nice young thing from the midwest

Drugs
I hate you
I hate all the things you do
You turn them into losers
Self maiming victims
Sleep walkers
Life is not tough enough to withstand civilization

I can feel it coming from far off
It starts to get to me
These clubs, the smell and the dim lights
Inside these places pieces of myself fall away
Layers peel off in Death's shade
Despair is like that
It grows and spreads
It's happening tonight, right now
As I sit and wait to destroy this place

A man sits next to a table in a small apartment
He has just fixed and shot up a dose of heroin
He will miss his shift at work and lose his job
New York boils and screams below

A man sits on a public bus on his way home from work. He is exhausted.
The bus is hot and the smell of human sweat is almost overpowering.
He thinks of the stranger he married, their child who will have cold
strangers as parents. He thinks that the last person that he would want
for a father would be himself. The apartment is too small and the walls
are too thin. Time is running out and things didn't turn out the way he
thought and hoped they would. Not as if he had a clue as to what it was
he was supposed to do with his life. No direction. Swept up in the winds
of carbon monoxide and pain. He stares at the floor and inhales. His
head explodes.

Rock Band
How can you hang around after shows and let these people stroke you

They'll make you weak
After you play, pack and head for the darkness
Crouch low in the bush and repair
Prepare your mind and body for the next engagement
What's all this standing around?
They are not your friends
No one is your friend
As soon as they figure you out, they dismantle you
And put you up on the shelf with their other broken toys
You have to hit and vanish
After I play I got nothing to say
I head back for the jungle, look at the stars and breathe deep
Inventory the damage and learn the lesson that was taught
I'm not interested in a social scene
These admirers of yours
As soon as they have you figured out they will destroy you

We were walking on a trail
You looked into my eyes and all you could see was jungle
There are some people that you can't get close to
You find that you can't find them
They hide themselves too well
Ones who paint the walls of their rooms with their eyes
Ones that fill endless hours of silence
With the sound of their breathing
Alone in any place, in any embrace
Beyond heartbreak
Beyond love and hate
Invisible people
Terminal strangers
We walk on time's outer crust
Enveloped in shadows
Encircled in pure jungle

Train through Indiana late at night
Wet streets reflect the glow of the lamps
I pass by at 75 mph
It's like a pass a moth makes at a flame
Sometimes it's all you get

Be careful with your face
Be careful with your eyes

Be careful with what you say
You can't retract a single thing you do
Every action is true
Some people don't care about apologies
When you lose your temper
You throw in all your cards
You give them everything they need to pull you apart
Be careful with what you let show
Be careful with what you hold back and how you do it
Some people can read faces like headlines

It's getting near 3 AM
This room is hot, the air is damp and going nowhere
I am thinking of her
Whenever my mind sets to wander at night
It goes to thoughts of her
It was so long ago that I have forgotten almost all the facts
And replaced them with lies to fill in the gaps
The truth is a rough road to her front door
The truth tore holes in me
I lie to myself in this room
Except for the worst parts, my mind refuses to cover them up
They twist the knife alright
Life is a fucked up deal
Full of traps and snares
The more I go on
The more I want to put a bullet through my head
Sometimes it's the only thing that makes sense
But then the lies creep in
And keep me hanging in for another beating

After a while life isn't so hot
I got to a certain age
And saw that I was competing
With the 22 year old version of myself
Checking the mirror to see if I still looked good
Like I did when I didn't have to try so hard
I do things now to see if I can still do them
Back then I was a genius
I'm smarter than that now
I have to work hard at what was easy
I have to look hard to see new things

It used to be that that was all I saw
I'll have to work harder on that one
—◊—

Hot black night wrapped around me
Breathing in ink, swallowing me whole
Like jumping into a pool of black water
Moonlight scarring its surface
Stab wounds of moonlight
My tunnel vision brain
War heat insanity, the way to go
Beyond
A soldier into the void
Terminate the sun
—◊—

I sleep on floors of people's houses
Always moving, always displaced
I was walking down this road today before soundcheck
I was thinking about this endless shuffle
Always moving
A lifelong haul
I'm a constant stranger
But I always know where I am
Always moving
—◊—

This life is putting lines in my face
A limp in my step and gravel in my voice
They come up to speak to me
I don't feel human
I feel like I have been beamed down to spread a new disease
It runs me ragged
—◊—

I hate to think of you
I hate the memories
They always lead up to the part where you dumped me
Last week you sent me a letter
Telling me that you have been thinking about me
And how you want to be my friend
Your beauty is a disease
A sharp blade that keeps cutting night after night
Scar tissue is stronger than normal flesh
You are turning me into a living scar
I don't know whether to thank you or myself
—◊—

The great emptiness
After the show is over
I come out on the stage to load out the gear
An hour ago the place was full of people and noise
I look up at the roof
I can see the ghost of the music
All of a sudden it all seems so futile
I feel empty like the dance hall
I feel wooden like the floor
When the equipment is loaded out
And the exit door has been slammed shut behind us
I feel extinct

In these places I see them
Dead drunks
Choking on the booze
Tiny pig eyes that squint to check me out
Ugly and fat, waiting for Death
They bang their glasses and yell
When they are told to shut up, they do
They are broken
Spirits stomped to Death by dirty shoes
The urinal stinks all the way to the entrance
All the way back to their hovels
The way they look
I don't think they know it's happy hour

Tonight you smell gunpowder in the air
The street sounds are ripping through your head
You think about killing yourself as you stare at the ceiling
Ignore it
It's just a tiny disease that the city gave you
The streets give you poison dreams
Little seeds that sprout in your mind
Everything starts to talk to you
Sirens sing to you, brakes call out your name
The water pipes chant
It's hard not to hear it when they speak so clearly to you
You can't tell anybody
They don't know what you're going through
But you and I know
Don't let the cities fool you

You see how they glitter and lie
The glass eyed women who chew you up and spit you out
They leave you cut and broken in spirit
The filthy air fills your lungs with fire
The eternal hell of your room
They speak to you in rational tones
Be careful of yourself
—◦

I am despair
Didn't we meet in that dark doorway?
When your legs
Felt like they were going to give way like old crutches?
Yes, we saw eye to bloodshot eye that night
I make the walls breathe
I am cold and clammy and hot as tears
When you feel your soul splintering
You'll know I'm with you
Your friend in the shadows
That strikes like the viper
Holds like the pit bull
And drains like the leech
—◦

Are you still alive?
Open your eyes upon this summer blackout
You know the summers are scarring us
Year after year they drag us down the molten streets
The sunsets burn down our backs
I was out tonight, looking at the blinking moaning city
I know you're out there somewhere
I wonder if you're thinking what I'm thinking
Do you ever think about you and me
And the summer nights we passed through?
They were some of the best times of my life
I inhale this night
It always smells the same and it fills me with longing
Do you ever sit outside and look into the black heat
And think about this?
Do summer nights ever break your heart?
—◦

The guy in the opening band was asking me a lot of questions
I was sitting on a stool smelling my sweat turn to ammonia
I was telling him there was no money in this

Just a lot of work and missed sleep
But at the end of the day you get to play
I listened to myself talk as I watched the sweat run down my legs
I had been playing this club for years
Probably while this one was in junior high
I told the guy that he better get used to it
If he could hang with that, then it would be a great time
Now I'm sitting in this restaurant waiting for the food
It's getting in near 4 AM
This trip is destroying me
But at the end of the day I get to play

Pain is mother father teacher friend
Tonight my body was trying to kill me
Pain was surging through my body
I am addicted to pain
Pain is the highest order
Love never stays
Pain never leaves
Always did right by me
Never lied

I'm on the floor of some guy's house
I don't know his name, I call him "Hey Man"
I smashed my nose playing tonight
Bled all over myself
Now I'm here all crashed out with two people snoring next to me
I look at my dirty pillow
I see new and old blood stains
All mine
I had a sheet awhile ago
It had a lot of blood on it
A girl bled on it one night in I forget where
Nice girl anyway
My nose hurts and I'm all alone
Sleeping on a mildewed sheet
My back and knee are in pain's embrace
I got no complaints
Except I wish we got out on the road earlier this year
Good night

I'm the straight man

Walking with a slight limp down crooked streets
I am the set up man
Your jokes fly by my head
They aren't funny
They don't penetrate the skin, skull or anything else
What do you look like turned inside out?
Put your hand in a vice and crank it tight
Speak the truth like a dog speaks the truth
I'm a bit worn down from the process of definition
At the bottom of your eyes I find a shaking uncertainty
I know you by your cracks and infirmities
They shine like badges
I eye you calmly
There's nothing you can do that doesn't warn me

Waiting
The guy in bed alone waiting for the angel
What the fuck is on your mind?
There's no one that will be able to reach you
No one to touch you and have it change you
That only happens in movies
Don't let these alien dreams destroy you
They just want you to buy more
They don't want to take your pain away
Then they wouldn't have a carrot to dangle in front of your face
Please run at full speed towards yourself

Backstage
I sat in the small room stretching my legs
I felt the fire shoot up my hamstrings
The carpet next to me was covered with vomit
I looked at the cigarette butts
I Read the stupid shit on the walls
Later after the show
I sat in the room and tasted the vomit in my mouth
People filed by the doorless door way to get a look
Like viewing the body
This is the way it is

What are you going to do?
Shoot me?
Oh, you're just going to talk

You're talking to a corpse
I've been dead to your world for years
What you say doesn't mean much to a stiff

My little friend 1-3
1: I wish I could help you
I wish I could love you
You die every night
One eyed silver express into your arm
Your blood is dead
I wish I could touch you
You're poison

2: I sit and wait for the sun to rise
Tonight is slow
Taking forever
I don't have forever to give
This night leaves wounds
I feel pins under my flesh
The night drags on
Slow mournful beauty

3: Take me with you
I don't care where you're going
I want to go with you
I want to see your eyes until I die
I never saw eyes so clear
They cut me

I used to sing myself to sleep
I was raised on my own voice
I would talk to myself on my paper route
When someone talks to me
I often answer myself back
I'm the one I have come to depend on
I figure the more self involved I become the better
On the outside, people will just wear you out
I write letters to myself
I wish there was a way to call myself on the phone
When I need to see a face that understands me
I look into the mirror
When I was growing up I would be alone in the apartment

I would talk to myself
Strangers are too strange
━◦

Bono
When I saw you in Westwood
I should have punched you out
Now I'm punching myself
For not taking advantage of a good opportunity
To express myself
As you walked quickly past
I could see that you were nervous
No bodyguards to save you from the animals of the streets
The ones you sing about from behind the tinted glass
I should have wasted you don't you think?
The one to destroy you
Would have made great copy for the shitheads at mtv
Watching the other fuck ups vying for your position
They would have shoved another Bozo band into your slot
Within minutes
I should have terminated your contract
I don't think you see how totally expendable you are
━◦

Tonight my thoughts go out to the woman
She has no name
Because she has all their names
I stare at a blank wall
I can see her face
My thoughts fly from my skull
They crash and burn in the night
I sit in the darkness as my soul starves
Every sense sharpens
I can articulate my starvation for touch
She becomes more beautiful
Her eyes burn brighter as the nights pass
Her features become clear
More nights pass
She starts to decompose
She wears away to black night still moving air
I starved her to Death
I destroyed that longing
━◦

Power Strength Destroy Exhaust Terminate Lie Despair Carnage

Incinerate Surge Rise Shine Burn Scatter Shatter Jungle Suicide
Insanity Force Regret Disease Rage Truth Reality Born Machine Kill
Mission Over
Until it breaks
Until it falls
Until it dies
Until it rots
Until it breathes life
Until it burns
Until it tells the truth
Until it gets real
Until it gets destroyed
Until it knows what it is
—+

All to the one that walks away
Back to the gleaming jungle alone
Only to emerge again stronger
Love sends him away
He gives from joy and malice
—+

My mother and father tried to kill me
I had to give birth to myself
I had to give myself to myself
Every night I have to re-create myself
I must be my inspiration
I recharge myself with myself
Self motivated, self involved, self contained
Who cares about me, you?
Right
I am all there is
—+

Woman in the hotel lobby
I smell your perfume as you walk by
I stare at the man you're with
I could take him out in a second
I see you and your clothes fall to the ground
I want to taste you
I would rip that guy out of the picture to get to you
You've been gone for 10 minutes now
The lobby still smells of your perfume
The night is cold and passing slow
I want to feel your flesh on mine

Tell me what I have to do

I thought I was in love with you but I was wrong
I fell through your eyes
Slipped through your embrace
You tried to hold on
I tried too, I swear
I fell and I'm still falling
Crashing through floors of a house in a burning dream

They're all over me
I smell their beer breath mixed with my sweat
I can't answer all the questions, I can barely think straight
Now I'm alone in the room
To be hard you must be alone
To withstand this shit you must be hard
The logic works itself out right in front you
Be alone as much as you can
If you want to hit like a ton of fire
You have to get to the essential number
One

Road
Looking out of the window of the van
It's night and we are speeding through Germany to Austria
I look out and see lights and fields
It could be Wisconsin
I think to myself as the lights strobe the median
This is my home
The road passing underneath me
The truckstops, the weary faces, the road, the movement
The miles slam through my eyes
Crease my face and harden my jaw
I can't think straight unless I'm moving
I sleep in hotels and on floors and I sleep soundly
The road is cold, lonely and true
It gives me life
One long road stretching out in front of me

Beautiful stranger
I see you looking at me
Come here please

I want to meet you
Are you lonely like me?
Displaced dislocated
Soul's back broken?
No one has looked at me like that for weeks
Blond hair, blue eyes, cautious smile
I see the mad crowd swirling around you
We held hands through that song
Until they tore us apart
I hope they didn't hurt you like they hurt me
Like I hurt myself
After the show I could hardly move
Tired, sweat pouring off me
I tried to get up to find you
It took too long to get through the people at the back
I knew it was futile, I knew you had gone
I went into the hall
It was so empty
Floor littered with plastic cups and trash
You were gone
10 million miles away
I never learned your name
I thought about you as I did two interviews
I kept seeing your face
Now I'm in a hotel room
A dungeon several layers beneath civilization's crust
I can't sleep
I keep seeing your face
The way you looked at me, so real
I watched you dancing with yourself
It looked like you were in your own world
Haloed in honeyed hair
Your eyes are glued to mine
Solitude hurts right now
The room is small and getting smaller
Maybe someday I'll meet you
I'll be back if I am not destroyed in the mean time
I'll be back, look for me
I want to know how you taste
How it feels when your body is pressed against mine
p.s.
When that guy threw the cigarette

That landed on my back, stuck and burned
You were the only one that noticed
I could live for years in the way your eyes looked at me

I started stalking Death
More beauty, more light, more power
Get up and show me something
I started stalking Death, living all the time
New pain, newer, brighter, burning
Mutation, evolution in my zone
Do it, pull it
What the fuck are you going to do, kill me?
I stalk Death
Moving forward, shaking life
Through animal driven eyes

I have no problem with hostility
I was raised with it
I was taught to be hostile or be destroyed
The other night when you threw the lit cigarette
The hostile brother came out
Last night when you tried to fuck with me
I sent you to the hospital
You sent me to the police station
As I was sitting with the pigs
I was thinking that I'm not fit for society
You tease the animal and it smacks you
You can't handle so you call the police
You make me lose control

I find myself dislocated
I don't know where to get off
My heart has broken so many times that it won't do it anymore
Am I dead?
Don't answer, don't write, don't say anything
I haven't heard it all, I've heard enough

In these brutal times honesty leaves scars
I can see why so many of them stand in line and lie
I can see what the truth has done to me
I'm not as old as I used to be
I feel farther away from them now

Than when I hated them all

What does it take
Do I want to know
Do I care anymore
Can I say that the scars on my hands don't exist?
From all the times I reached out
Can I say that I like it anymore?

When I go outside I feel stupid
I look at them and I can't see the reason I'm here
It's like being in a bad movie
So I stay in the room and wait to go back on the road again
I went out to see a show tonight
As I pass people I hear them say my name
I run back to them and ask them what they want
They look at me like I live in a museum
I go back to the room and wait to leave again
I don't get it
This place rejects me

Waiting at the bus stop on Santa Monica Blvd
Cars pulling over to check out my dick
I stand away from the curb so I don't get confused with meat
Besides, it's easier to dodge the bullets
I was in a club waiting to see a band
But they were going on so late I couldn't take it anymore
Having to look at people trying to look cool
As they die from boredom
On the way out I heard this guy give the bouncer a raft of shit about the
wait in the line. The bouncer told him that there was nothing he could
do. The guy kept it up and the bouncer got mad and said that he was
having a bad night and he'd love to take it out on his narrow white ass.
I thought that was a great line.
I look at the others waiting for the bus
Dull and covered with LA's spit
No place on earth bakes and destroys them like here
This is the alienator land
You have to learn the prison shuffle
It's the only way to get along
It all looks like a jail to me
I look at the skinhead with the incredibly ugly girlfriend

They start to kiss violently
Where the hell do you think they started out from
Where are they going
What are their dreams
Human machines getting the life squeezed out of them
I don't want to go out like this
I don't want to go out near this desert hell

Where are you tonight my loneliness?
I sit in my room
I keep the music loud to distract my mind
There was a woman here last night
It was hard to not walk out in the middle of the whole thing
Where is the echo in my heart?
Will I ever meet someone
That will take the bitter taste from my mouth?
I am loneliness
I wish I had someone to miss

Show business
You watch out there son, don't let them dissect you
They'll ask you a million questions
They'll want to know everything
You'll think that they want to know because they like you so much
Let me tell you the truth
The minute you tell them everything
You'll be more alone than a poor man with a social disease
You'll never see them again until you read their version of you
They'll always try to figure you out
So they can see where the hell you get off
The bottom line is that they don't like you
In fact they hate your guts
Don't let'em pull your pants down
They'll be so done with you
The vacuum they leave as they run to the next sucker
Will suck the sweat right out of your pores
Don't let'em love you too much either
You remember that old saying:
You always hurt the one you love
Well son it's true
The minute they love you, look out!
They'll tear you to pieces...

They want a little piece to take home
Hell son, that's why they invented t-shirts!
Always make them hate you just a little bit
Just to keep'em coming back
But not so much they want to hang your knee caps off the rear view
Always keep'em guessing son
Tell'em you're an artist, works every time
The less sense you make the more they'll like you
That's show business son

Watch out, they're weak and all over the place
Every day you have to get power
Otherwise they will destroy you
They can't help their weakness
The only way not to become a walking casualty
Is to learn as much as you can about yourself
That's the first thing they try to do
They try to take you away from yourself
They will try to blind you to yourself
If you try to find out who you are
They'll call you self-centered
They're mad that you no longer work for them
 If you relent
They come in and fill you full of shit
All I'm saying is that you have to be careful

Cowards
They all want to hear the word "we"
They fill stadiums to hear the word "we"
They don't like to hear the singular voice
They fear themselves
They hide in the cancerous folds of unity
They breed fear into everything they do
Life is so short
You might as well be yourself
I will do this crazy thing
No sell out, I'll see what happens
I will rage to the end

Alien boy
He was ugly
It gets worse

He has bad skin, is too smart and sensitive for his own good
He lives in the mid west, Russia, Paris, you name it
He feels it
The silence of his room
The occasional rage
The desire to touch
Sometimes it gets to be too much
He claws at his flesh
He's everywhere
I saw him last night at a show
He told me about the writers that he likes
I could tell from the way he was describing them
That these books were saving his life
I get letters from him all the time
They don't understand him in Berlin
He can't identify in Portland
He can't get the courage to talk to a woman in New York
He tells me about the music he likes
His favorites never come to Mississippi, N. Dakota or Alabama
He says he lives in his room
He writes a lot
Maybe he'll send me some if I want to see it
Alien boys, rock steady

Behind the ivy:
We gave you the money, now do it right
We'll close our eyes, hurry
Make a miracle, I'll have my television on
I'll watch at 7 &11 to see how you did
I don't know what needs fixing
I don't know what needs stopping
I don't know the right names and I don't care
It's not my job to know anything
Don't go away, but leave me alone
Don't get any funny ideas
Some people have been hired to watch you
We don't know them, but they know you
And they know what you're supposed to be doing
So you better get it right, otherwise they'll tell us
And we'll hire someone to tell them to tell you
That you better be doing what you're supposed to be doing
Now I don't know what that is, but someone does

I think
—•

I want to thank you
You taught me not to need or want you
I took the lesson and went on
You forced me into myself
You made me see myself
I learned not to depend on anyone for anything
I remember you told me all this stuff
About how you needed me
I took it all in
I wanted to be with somebody
And then you took it all back
It's all a lie
A commercial for something
So now I'm out here in the free zone
It's no ghetto
—•

They are not deserving of my hate
I don't hate them
I hate the disease that's eating them alive
I hate the thing that makes them what they are
I hate the machine that causes them so much pain
My hate is a grand scale machine
A full and wonderful event
Not to be squandered on some punk
Some weak powerless fear victim
No
I'm taking mine to a higher place
—•

12.2.88 12:58 AM LA, CA:
I walk down the street to dump the last of the day's mail
The air smells like something huge has died near by
Maybe everyone in the city died and no one told me
I see a couple looking into their car
It got broken into
There's safety glass on the sidewalk
I was in the studio all day
7 hours of listening to myself
My body hurts
I have band practice early in the morning
I called a girl tonight, to make some contact

I'm still wondering why I did something so stupid
She put me in my place
I know better now
Like I really have something to say to a girl
I cross the street
I see several girls leaving a club
I think of a man sitting in his room
He puts a gun in his mouth and pulls down
He hangs himself
He lies in bed with a beautiful woman
Whenever I see this pitiful stretch of Sunset Blvd
Bathed in crime lights
I know that I'm in the deadest place on earth
It's where dreams come to die
My house is right up the street

Last night playing that show in LA
The pain got me good
My entire body was consumed
Every movement I made was accompanied by a cramp
By the last song I could barely stand up
I fought myself to stand up straight
I could feel my body rebel
My own body turning against me in front of strangers
I went backstage and sat in a corner
My legs felt so fucked that I didn't trust them to stand
That's my religion, power through pain
Today I woke up sore and strong
The other day this woman told me
I was wrong negative and violent
I couldn't make her see where I was coming from
I would rather die than take all the shit she does at her job
I would rather lose the whole thing tomorrow than sell out

This night puts another tumor in my brain
I can feel myself caving in a little every time I breathe
Every night here moves slow
The air is hot, vacant and fake
Crime lit, violent, diseased
Where the hell can I go?
I don't think I could handle a place I didn't hate

The boy calls me late at night to talk to me
I am his best friend, his only friend
I am the only one who understands
That's how it is with strangers

Alien song
Where do I fit in?
It must be a place I've never been to
I don't understand what they are saying
They don't make me feel anything
I can't get close
I don't know where to go
I stay inside my head
Words choke me
I've learned to destroy parts of myself
I kill the parts that feel
I'm afraid of them
I feel like I must be a different species
I feel lonely but I'm working to get rid of that
I'm working hard not to want anything from their world
It's hard going, but I'm getting better all the time
Sometimes I feel like I'm falling
Sometimes I feel like I'm on ground so solid
Back to the wall with all the answers
Having seen heard and felt enough of their world
I am alien

Do you remember the last time
The great crash, the big depression
The one that felt like a storm had ripped through you
And left four days of mud in your guts
Maybe you were in your room
Nothing made sense
You couldn't hide from yourself
Something came in
And stole all the parts of your brain that didn't hate you
Self doubt was coursing through your veins
Do you remember that one?
Nothing worked
You tried playing your good records
The ones that got you through the last one
Iggy, Lou, The Godfather of Soul

The real thing
Even they couldn't get you out of the hole
You couldn't think of one thing to change the situation
All of a sudden you didn't know yourself anymore
You started hating the stranger you were alone in the room with
Do you remember that one?
Me too

The memories come and wash pain, sadness and regret over you
They have sharp eyes that stare into yours without flinching
They cut ugly shapes into your flesh
The night moves slow like your oncoming Death
Like a car crash that won't quit
Can you forget, can you get rid of it?
You're left with no choice but to deal with yourself
The memories track you down like assassins
You're amazed at the cruelty you inflict upon yourself
You're some kind of criminal
You hold your head in your hands
Feeling for the on-off switch

Picture this
You're walking down a long hallway
On the walls are many pictures
Pictures of people you know
Pictures of yourself
All the good times
They taunt you with their silent stares
They start to talk to you all at once
You walk faster, trying to get away
It doesn't matter how fast you walk, the pictures won't stop
You recognize the faces the places, the times, all the things you were
All the things you were thinking.
You hear yourself say:
I love you, I'm never going to die, I want to kill myself
You can't escape your life
You scream, you want to be someone else, something else
Someone without a face, without a name
Someone that never knew anyone, who never felt the pain
Someone that didn't have to exist all the time
Your history becomes your enemy
You run, you fall exhausted

But in your ears and eyes
The times that will never leave and never come back
They all come crashing in on you
Your body feels like a prison
You start to drown in yourself
Where to now
—◦

There was this guy
He ran out of stuff
One night he was sitting in his room and it occurred to him
That he was totally empty
He didn't love or hate anyone or anything
He thought of all the women he had been with
The times he was full of fear
Ready to fight or die
Seemed like a long time ago
Seemed like it had happened to someone else
And he had merely read about it
The more he thought about it
The more he thought that it was all a big joke
A big to-do over nothing much
He remembered all the time he spent in anger
He felt like he had wasted his life being a monumental ass
It was a big game and he had been walking through it like it was real
Like it was real life
All that bullshit was nothing
He felt nothing
He never felt better
—◦

Strung out looking for a friend
Feeling sick, no one understands
You're a hero in disguise
Monkey chewing on your ear
Your body and its vile needs
Call a ghost on the phone
All of your friends have become strangers
You mutated, dipping low, lower
A race for the bottom
You're the only one on the trail
Grey sky, cold walls
Everything sounds like WWIII in a cement mixer
They never did understand
—◦

There will be no Valhalla for you
There will be the television set and the beer
Waiting for you like a trap
There will be no glory
There will be re-runs and ulcers
There will be sleepless nights
Looking at all the women and thinking
Regrets hopes and dreams
The thoughts of a fighter on his way down
But you threw the fight
There will be no real life
There will be the alcohol circus
The sadness, the jealousy
There will be nothing at the end of your line
Except maybe a commercial
Father

You electrify me
Your eyes lock me in
The war is roaring in my ears
I fell time pass through me
Turn me into living electricity
Up, more
I can't get enough
Maybe you should kill me
Maybe you should give me too much
Until I overload
Electrify me

The noise they make sends me running
Sends me running and makes me feel alone
Their words hit me like hammers
Don't look, don't see me
Don't hurt me with your recognition eyes
You don't know how much it hurts
Don't talk to me
It reminds me of the distance
The cold room, the window I look through
The echo in my heart
The shallowness of my world
My cowardice
I like you

Don't tell me your name
Don't touch
I break too easily

City
I will kill you
I will kill all of your friends
I will run them down like I'll run you down
Doesn't matter what you do
I don't sleep
I live to kill you
I am an institution, a way of Death
Think of how napalm sticks and burns
I will hunt you, stalk you
I will infect your dreams
I will make you want me, need me
I will make you love me and then I will kill you
I am the definition of relentless
I win, you lose, always
I keep you plugged into my life support system
And then I cut you off
You die like some creep
Withered, polluted and destroyed
Give me your children, they taste good
So strong, so stupid
Me, so hungry, so beautiful
The perfect killing machine
I invented suicide
I am the ultimate disease
I suck the blood right out of you
You thank me for it
The sun never sets on my empire
Thanks to you, I work

I am not in a state of confusion
I don't get hung up on emotion
My coldness will freeze the tears off your face
I see what love does to you
I see you drinking yourself into the floor
I see you destroy yourself
You try to deny your hate
You put it below you

You become a stranger and an enemy to yourself
See you in the real world
—+

I walk these streets
I see you
You don't see me, I'm a stranger
I see the desperate war you have going on
I walk the streets and observe
You hide your fear and call it something else
You're addicted to all the things that make you weak
I work hard to get your filth away from me
For awhile, your fake pain was all I had
Your words are antiques
Your movements are but gestures
You have made this place small and dirty
That's the way of the weak
The blind leading the crippled to the cliff
And then charging money to let them jump
You make suicide illegal so you can make a buck on misery
Your circus stinks
Fuck it
The storm is coming
—+

The days go on, I see them fall away
They tell me why I should follow them on the burnout path
It seems like internal drive is a disease
I thought they were like me
I see that I'm wrong
All I can do is get on with it
If you want to get things done
Stay away from people
They'll slow you down and break your heart
—+

Things are different now
They guard themselves and distance themselves
They used to confront, now they hide
They have cultivated arrogance
I see through it
It's hard to see them retire before they're dead
At the end of the trail all hearts will be broken
All promises will be crushed
All bones will be turned to dust
—+

I just spent 3 days and nights with a woman
I thought it was going to be different
I cannot get close to anyone
I have lost the ability to lie to myself
I've never felt farther away from the human race
May be I'm too selfish
Too shallow
So full of shit that I can't understand myself
When she left I was confused and alone
I wished I never met her
Soon I felt better knowing I was on my own
Sometimes the sound of my own voice makes me want to kill myself
—◆

Tour is starting soon and they have a lot of questions
I have to be all of history
I have to be stronger than all of their worlds
I have to take the weight of their fear
I have to take it in silence
I cannot blow up in their faces
I have to take them down the trail
In my darkest hour I come to rescue myself
Sometimes I wonder what the hell is on their minds
What it all means to them
Sure as hell is different than it is for me
—◆

Every day the distance inside me grows
It feels good
I can't count the times emotion got in the way of work
Now I'm breaking away from them
Deeper into myself
I'm black hole inside myself
A dark jungle
Nothing will ever get me out of here
I can run wild and not think of them at all
So many times I have hurt myself at their expense
Sold out to their human values
That's how they kill you
They enslave you to their weakness and then they make you love it
I get farther away every day
I see clearly from this high perch so deep inside
Destroy
—◆

Tonight I am not alone
I'm in the company of pain
Pain is my brother, my friend, my guardian
When pain is with me I know that I'm alive
Pain is the great teacher
The self affirmer
Pain makes me see
Only through pain do I get power
The more pain I endure the stronger I get
When they come I am ready
When it comes time I am always ready
I taste my blood regularly
Hail pain

Your words can't hold me down
Your love and hate mean nothing to me
I answer to a much higher order
True order
I can't talk to you without seeing through
You only go so far and then you turn back
War all the time
Streets exploding, airstrikes at night
The palms waving with flame
I'm in solitary
I have a long way to go before I am called in
You might think me cold
Perhaps you should forget me

That man locked in a cage
Pure animal
screaming: I'll kill you all
I need to be locked in a cage
The less I have the better
That's why I don't want you to touch me
Tenderness makes me weak
I should be made to crawl everyday
To strip myself of will
Will destroy me
That mean ass animal
Tear your eye out and shove it down your throat
I need to caged
The more animal the better

They wouldn't understand
One must depend on one's self
—•

In a hole, in a trench
I will not stop
They would like to see me destroyed
For me the night explodes
I have snakes of steel underneath my flesh
My blood propels me
They can't decode me
I am the solitary discipline
I give all to the command
I am an instrument of the iron voices
Attack
Destroy
Love only your weapon
Self made
She was so beautiful so fake so full of shit
The roaring jungle in my veins
I can't hear you
All I can hear is myself dying
—•

I fly like a vulture over the fires of creation
I am Part Animal Part Machine
Howling mekanikal
My existence pushes me forward
There is only one way for me
You will never know me
—•

I watch the music play
I watch the fat liar with the untouchable money
These bands take all the people that like them
To a place that bleeds painlessly
And then there are people like me
People that you throw peanuts at
I see you, yes I do
I must endure your shallowness daily
How can you lie to yourself like that
How can you go for this shit?
Fuck it, I am the all the time war man
This guy told me I should take some time out to smell the roses
I am the things that you deny

I am all the things that you hate the world for
I wish I wasn't alive as much as you are dead

Heroin
Coke
Speed
I hate you
I hate what you do to women's faces
I hate what you do to their breasts
I hate what you do to their bodies
But most of all I hate what you do to their minds
You turn women into witches and worse
The girl gives me the same junked out story
She probably looked good once
She loves the needle
She can't get away
Like the woman who wanted to fuck me the other night
Re-habbing from coke
What a joke
No one gets away
Coke is all she talked about
How she doesn't do it anymore
I can spot drugs on a woman a mile away
I hate drugs

That thing you just saw me do wasn't entertainment
I was just injecting the freak disease into you
I get off on myself
I freak out on myself
I have nothing for you to take
I give what is destroying my mind and body
There's no place for me except this cage
I used to try to explain myself
I wanted to be like you
I washed extra hard to be clean and perfect
I fell into myself and here I am
I have been spared the human hell
I have one of my own

I am the freak that wants to touch you
I have a disease that I want to give you
Loneliness and insanity

Glimpses of the Abyss
Let me turn you on
Let me turn on you
Feel the touch
Stranger on your flesh, on your breath
We are cold and on our way to Death
I have something I want to give you
Let me mutilate you and look the other way
—

Ignite
Turn on
Explode
Yell
Jump
Kill yourself
Die trying
Hate
Destroy something
Are you alive?
Do you feel anything?
Do you think you have 1000 years to live?
Are you...
Forget it
—

I'm in a room alone
Getting ready for all the cities
The flesh is weak but the mind is strong
This is it
The bullet passes once
I catch it in my teeth
Tonight
—

I can smell my sweat
I just worked out and jerked off
And now I want to kill something
I think it's better that I keep to myself
In my brain I see fire lightning power and Death
I am drawn inwards
I hear the voice inside clearer than anything else
I have to stay strong
I live for the pain
I want to see where it falls

I want to see where it lies
To pull myself towards Death
That is my dream
I will document my breakdown and destruction
—◦—

1.2.89
Ugly machine
Take me up
Pull me into your giant cylinder
Tear me up
Reduce to the component parts
Show me what I'm made of
I want to know
—◦—

I saw the pigs take him away
All of a sudden he was like some kind of star
—◦—

The woman in the jar
Her friends gathered in a circle
To wish her well into the next world
The woman in a jar dead a week
Cancer
It was a clear day
I could see the Hollywood sign
—◦—

He told me that his brother
Had shot himself in the head with a shotgun
Left no note
—◦—

I have problems with the way you look at me
You remind me of myself
It's a bad picture
Do you ever feel trapped?
—◦—

She painted a picture in her mind
Of how it should be
When reality hit her
It broke all the windows in her room
She found a new life inside herself
She was wrapped up with no way to get out
All she had was a one way ticket to her insanity
It keeps her warm at night
—◦—

For years they had me locked in a cage
They told me to be proud of what I was
And what they thought it made me into
They tried to teach me to love the cage
And to love them
It didn't work
—◦—

He got punched in the guts
He fell to his knees
Later he would call it a rite of passage
—◦—

Love's Theme
Thank you for letting me live inside you
For allowing me to tell you how you feel
I'm in the construction-destruction business
I build you up
Tie you into my life support system
Then I pull the plug and step back
I watch you consume yourself
When I see the tears fall from your eyes
I know I've done my job
What the fuck did think this was, Real Romance Monthly?
I like it when you come down with my disease
I like it when you become me
That's how I find out about you
All those nights you had me in your arms
You see now that you never had anything
Look at the way I have permanently disfigured you
Look at the scars that I leave
Thanks again
I'll be back even though you say you hate me
—◦—

These hotel rooms
Lost rooms
Every night a new place to sleep
Re-enforce the emptiness
Clarify the alienation
The nights rip by
Layers of distance coat my brain
These sterile un-lived in rooms
Stacked, looking over the neon sprawl
Terminal jet lag
—◦—

Her nipples pushing high against her shirt
Triumphant, forcing the issue
—•

The old men drink, bellow, croak and laugh
Then recede into darkness
—•

She was lost
She turned to strange men
Strange drugs
She found new and bitter tastes in her mouth
The city wrapped around her like a snake
Shrink-wrapped itself to her pores
She went down for the count
—•

The fields of pain have opened my eyes
Riding Death's highway to the end of the line
A brutal dream has been inflicted upon me
A darkness runs through me
This evil life
I have found ways to mutilate you
To make you show your true colors
I see you dancing without a brain
Mindless energy multiplying like car wrecks
I poke my fingers into you
Ball you up and throw myself away
An alien is born free and burning
The poison desert sings tonight
Slamming wind and metal together
The sparks fly and it's real
I learn from what was
I hear music in the ruins
I find harmony in the ashes
The safety is off
The One is straight ahead
—•

Something pathetic:
After several weeks on the road under strained conditions
Human kindness is scarce
Not that it ever really existed
I need the lie more than usual
It gets to the point where
If a waitress smiles at me, I melt

Need makes me weak and strong at the same time
It makes me hate my own guts
Some of the things I've done are hilarious
A waitress asked me if the food was good
I said yes and thank you 3 times
She laughed in my face
A girl asked me how I was doing
It took me 2 minutes to answer
It was 1 min 59 secs more than she wanted to know about
It's better when I keep my mouth shut

Anything for a rockstar
I was wrong, I thought you were different
I let down my guard
I thought it was your kindness that was drawing me out
I was just walking the plank
Talking like a fool trying to get it all out of me
Peeling my skin off and cutting myself to pieces
And then you asked me if I wanted a ride to the hotel
I said ok
You said: Anything for a rockstar
It became clear that you were just another one of them
You put a quarter in the talk box
I was a good evening of human entertainment
Now you can tell your friends
You're all the same to me

Decay
Weakness falling inwards
Pushed up against the wall
Alcohol disease
Too stupid for reality
The booze gives you the soft edges
The throat waiting to get cut
Tonight I watched you crash slowly
So this is the place you picked for your slow Death
Ah, fuck it
Just shut up and drink
Your life's not much

In Brisbane Australia
Backstage

A large cockroach runs through my clothes
The room is lit with florescent bulbs
The opening band is almost finished
Out there, about 200 people
Drunks walking in circles
There's a mirror over the sink
I can see my face spotted with rust
Sometimes, like right now
I feel empty as the hull of an old boat
Just a ribcage waiting to play
Sometimes I feel like such a goddamn fool
—

I walk the streets of my home town
Look at some of the places I used to live
I see someone that I knew a long time ago
What happens with age?
Because that shit means nothing to me now
I see all the people that never moved an inch in 10 years
I should feel nostalgic for this place?
That strangles and hypnotizes?
Fuck this thought, this backwards poison movement
It's not a nice home to hang your hat
It's all bones and cobwebs, Death and stillness
A lie trying to dance twice to the same tune
—

She is beautiful and strange
I catch a brief instant of her perfume
My imagination runs wild
Dances, explodes into flame
She does it perfectly
Her exactness and adherence to detail is excruciating
I look at her mouth, her neck
The force of her motion as she walks by
She's so natural at passing me by
She makes me feel extinct
Her beauty destroys me
As she walks away
She was born to destroy
She walks through the plate glass window of my heart
She doesn't get a scratch
As far as she knows
I don't exist
—

Every night on this road
A perfect ugly brutal blade
Stabbing hacking, deciding that what is, is
A good night rips its claws down your back
You feel this beast
And you know you'll miss it when it's gone
You'll go looking for it somewhere else
In someone else
In your broken knuckles or bleeding mouth
Getting off, getting out
Getting onto the next one
Pull yourself from one to the next
Line to line, vine to vine
You're swinging now, singing now, bleeding now
Time never ends, it just finishes you
Recline on this beautiful mattress of endless feeling
You haven't fallen until you can't get up
You aren't beaten if you can still take a beating
The night is my friend because it's always here
Or on its way
Gotcha
—◦—

Ripped out of a silence
He asked me over the phone about the things I said
About scarification, mutilation and surrendering to the elements
It's impossible to explain anything
That anyone would want explained
I see beauty in the eye of brutality
I like scars on women
Show me your road map honey
Sing me your song
The truth is in the scars
No it's not ugly, it's beautiful
It's pure luck
It's the definition of fortune
To find yourself in a situation that you have to survive
I had nothing to say to this guy
I helped us both out and hung up
—◦—

My eyes grow clearer as I walk the trail
I cut through the thick jungle searching for the beauty
That will fill my shoes with my blood

No, I'll do it myself
It will be my tiny statement
My extension, my grasp
My elbow will snap broken
Don't you feel it, the need to cut deep
The urge to stalk
Discipline, strength, straight lines
Silence, stealth, calculation
Discrimination and the lunge
There's nothing to explain
You have no questions for me
But you have questions filling your pockets
Destroy them one by one
Eat them, fuck them, enjoy them
But answer them yourself
—◦—

Nijmegan Holland
Forgotten thrown away
Cold raining outside
Hendrix blasting this bar
An asshole in the corner hands pounding the bar off time
I was here 5 years ago
Watched these guys beat each other up
It was more interesting than the set
Soon the hash bar will open
Grubby nicotined fingers will deal to grubby nicotines fingers
The night will close in damply
Like a slow moving coward
Another show, another stop on the train
Romance quit, got a real job
Pouring beer and coffee
In a building covered with spray paint
Look at all these people who traded in life for this
Lives lightly crumpled
Placed gently in the garbage
Not decadent
Just lazy and indifferent
Crumbling, teeth falling out
Trying to look cool
As the whole thing passes them by
—◦—

Cockroach 20th Century Fox

After we have destroyed their world
We'll come out of our holes and meet again
You'll wrap yourself around me
After the storm has cleared
We'll find each other
In the new jungle, in the new garden
After the storm, we'll crawl out of our holes and start again
We'll take back what was ours to begin with
We are the true masters of the earth
We rise so strong
We are perfection
They destroyed themselves

Wheels and Wings
I walked down the ramp into the plane
London to Frankfurt, raining outside
Traveling alone eyes aching
5 subways shut down barely made the flight
Put on my head phones and put on a soul music compilation
Almost cried into my coffee
Looked at my face in the bathroom mirror, exhausted
I'm so tired, so lonely
I think of what I would say if I was with a woman
I'm so burned out, the only person I can stand is myself
I'm the only one I would put through this
Wheels and wings
The ride is everything
I'm all I've got
I'm all I can take
Another day has destroyed part of me
So far so good

Montreal
I'm a ghost shuffling through these hallways
Train stations, endless tracks
In and through nights
Tunnels of shrouded walkways
Silent roaring separates me from all lives
Up flights of stairs, in lines
They don't know me
I'm a ghost
Through these dying cities I float

The Blvds of whores
Needle parks
Looking for where the freak show's at
Finding myself there, meeting their eyes
Re-affirming the distance
Widening it, strengthening it
The more I see, the more I know, the deader I get
I don't exist sometimes
Times like right now
In this hotel room
Not wanting for anyone
Killing futility by starving it
I fed it to itself
I wait for daybreak to move to the next space
━◦

One way conversation
Yea, hi I thought I'd check in
This house I'm at is full of bugs
There's lots of things that I don't tell you
Lots of things that don't have words to wear
The light in this place is really bad
I'm thinking about your eyes
Hell, we're tied up in this shit you know
Stuck behind walls, frozen in doorways
I hope these bugs don't get into my food
If I could remember where I was
I could tell you where I'm at right now
I'm in someone's apartment that's all I know
I spent the night talking to a lot of people from a stage
I don't know who I am
A voice, an answering machine
One lining it through life
Yea sure I'm hung up, aren't you?
━◦

Chicago Bus station
Waiting on the 6 PM to Fort Wayne Indiana
Lines of people
A lot of them with pillows
The PA system booming
Jacksonville, Lexington, Richmond, Atlanta, Dallas, Hell
Destinations days away
This place fills me with filth

On the top floor
I thought if I heard one more plea for money
My eyes would explode
But down here where the busses take off
Overheated, the smell of popcorn
She's telling them all about how she's been there all day
All the way from Appleton WI
Her kids all over the place screaming
11 years ago a man chased me and Ian through here
Never understood why, but it scared us good
The depression in these places
Can squeeze the marrow from your bones
The road, the distance, the people
It drills a hole into your brain
I've been here for hours
I left the house I was staying at
They were trying to get me to talk to them
I had nothing to tell them so I split
These rides coat me with distance
Make me mute
People ask me where I've been
I tell them here and there
I feel bored out
Fills me with pure blues
Another night shuffling through the hallways
Onwards to nowhere
Can't think of anyone I want to be with
Though still I'm lonely
The bus will be 30 minutes late
I will be late for this show in the middle of nowhere
It's going to be a long night

Yes it's getting to me
I want to pawn my eyes
The cities starve my sight into a corner
Sullen indifference is the result
I think of how you might smile at me
How you might kiss me
Some nights I want you so bad
My imagination is like a curse
Loneliness is like a curse and a gift

This torment is simple
It keeps me here
Door locked and the lights out

In my room for the first time in 71 days
Trying to unwind
Trying to get back to normal
Forgot what that's like
Falling into this room
Last night was good
I was in the Road's chokehold
Now everything is moving slow
A new chokehold as the night drags its feet

Strange stranger reaching out
Grabbing hold in this mindless blindness
I search and destroy for kindness
That sits in my imagination's mind
Across a burning field
Across a drenching jungle
Strange stranger strangely as you go
I've always never seen you
But you're the only one I know

Don't touch me
I'll feel too good
I'll fall apart
The only thing holding me together is my pain

You tell me you love me
I hang up the phone
I know I won't be able to talk to you again

5.25.89 Black Sabbath Day
What came first: Coffee or Hate
Playing Black Sabbath at hard volume
Watching fire being dropped from planes
It's frustrating
To not be able to go in and do a job that needs to be done
Sitting in my room alone getting walked on by decadent hippies
Held down by freaks
I told the lawyer:

Plan B, Plan B!!
She asked me what the hell Plan B was
I told her that was the one where I go to their house
And kick the hippy dogshit right out of them
Then they'll know what the deal is
Violence is the international language
Hostility and sexuality make everything go
Walk talk put out or get fucked up
She knew I was right
But she said that we had to use legal channels
Shucks, there ought to be a law
I never thought I would have record company hassles, you know the
story where the guy hates his label and moans about how they are
fucking him and his music up and you want to tell his to shut up and get
a life. I thought that I would somehow be spared this fate. I felt myself
so far removed from that world. It's a mistake to think that no bad shit
will ever happen to you.

I never thought I would have to get a lawyer and go through all this,
but here I am, waist deep in bullshit. Held down by the hippie scum
bags at Texas Hotel records. It is incredible to me that I owe them.
They take vacations and I owe them. They know they can do anything
they want.

All I can think of is violence. My thoughts are full of it. I imagine me
wounding them in broad daylight, taking them outside while they kick
and scream in terror and disbelief that no one will save them from a
brutal mutilation session. All I can do is wait, pity...

Willie Loman
You got sold out
Bad news for a salesman
You thought you were dancing
But you were just getting pushed down the line

3:30 AM
Another burnt wasted day closes out
I'm alone in my room
It's good company
When I don't sleep alone
I feel that I have somehow sold out
For me it's better this way
You have to get used to your own company
After you do things make more sense

I've got nothing to say, nothing to feel
I like being alone
Alien is as Alien does

I sit at every bus stop in the city
Trying to understand on all levels
The noise and dirt settles on me
Roaring motorists detached going nowhere
At night I listen to the sirens, helicopters
The strange television violence knifing through the air
The lazy, indifferent gunshots
That salt and butter our block to taste

Alone in my room late at night
Awhile ago there was a woman here
She talked a bunch of shit
I told her it was time to leave
She did
I think about the fucking freak show I'm caught in
Looking through a magazine
There's a woman drinking beer with a dog
Sometimes you have to deny the entire world access
These freaks
Busloads full
The world is full
The air is getting hotter
Brings me to a burning reality
Fuck the faceless
Plow through them
Drop the fire
Kurtz was right
He always was
He's the only one who had the right idea
He gave the gift
The message from the jungle
Keep breeding
The more you got, the more I want to burn
I saw you last night
Scabbed mouthed and dangerous
Like a lab experiment
What a joke all of this is
What a shallow grave you dig for yourselves

Swinging like a hinge
Slack jawed and glazed
I don't need video games
I've got you
—

Torn
On an edge
Between falling apart and winding up tighter than ever before
One hand on the phone
In need of a human voice
I'm cold, talk to me
The other hand in a fist
Feeling like it could crush the world like an insect
I need someone, no one
For a moment, a breath
And then it's over
I pound myself into submission
I wait for the next day to start
—

Show me your scars tonight
Break down in tears
Fall apart in my arms
I need something to hold me together
Come undone
Show me
I will heal your wounds
The deeper they are
The better you'll feel when I'm done
Life is such a bitter pill
They hurt you and they tell you lies
They try to destroy you, but not tonight
Not here with me
All the walls you have built around you
All the defenses you have to protect you from them
Let them fall like concrete clothing
I will hold you
I will listen
—

When the world wraps its iron hands around your throat
When the poison ink night nearly pulls you down
When no one thinks and feels like you do
When you think you're alone with your pain

When you know that you have nothing in common with any of them
Think of me
The Alien
I know how it feels to need speak but have no words
The need to scream and have no voice
We have a silent voice together
You and I sing the perfect painful harmony
Together alone
In our rooms, cells, lover's fierce embrace
We come from the same place
—❖—

Remainder man: This night will go away. It will give way to the day. It won't have the dignity to go out with a bang. It will fade into the dawn like a coward shrinking away from the fight. But now, tonight, I'm here breathing it all in. Lungfull, cupful, gut full. Walking through it, endlessly walking. This night will fade into their world, their zone. The time will become theirs. After that, another night will slam itself into my guts. In out like a slot machine. Like a fuck, like bad luck, like a ride to the same place. The nights come like slow wave music. I feel the night from far off. When the sun starts to take its seemingly endless leave, when it stops polluting my life with its brightness and warmth. Liquid night, to swim in the night, bathing in ink. I hyperventilate, trying to get as much night air into myself as possible, as humanly possible. What a shallow concept. Human anything, don't remind me, it hurts enough already. At night the phone becomes the magic tool, the voices of the night might call in. Tales of the day sound good, like the wreck that we survived and crawled away from, the beast that didn't eat us alive. The fools that didn't destroy us. At night we become secret and electric, open to suggestion and truth. It all looks good at night. Violent sexual and ultimate. You look good at night, you look like the only thing in the world that matters. Show me your dances of abandon. Let your hands outline my body, hurt me, scar me, make me remember you forever, turn into a lyric, a living dream. Right here in this night, in this deep place, in this high ceilinged crawl space.
—❖—

What, this hallway, this shuffle?
An endless series of doorways
All these strangers passing, passing
The idea of home
What a handout of an idea
What a vagrant lie
To think that we ever sit still

To think that we belong anywhere
You're telling me that this is the way it is?
You and I are the same
Tenants
Renters all
We are the ones given the task of passing time
Killing time
Getting away from ourselves
Getting away...
Another mongrel idea
An insult to life itself
No one gets away
Just lost, sidetracked, detoured
Success
Is the most distorted, insane, violent monster of an idea
Either you make it your life
Or you try not to laugh yourself to Death
Some people think
Their deeds will be written in stone forever
I don't know about deeds
It all looks like an act to me
Saying something to get to something else
Like the man who says I love you
By putting a gun in his mouth and pulling down
In making the connection we lose the connection
Losing
Perhaps the most honest thing we could ever do
The first loser must have been a genius
A true human pioneer
So tonight don't tell me of your great plans
Don't tell me of your journeys and the lessons learned
Your glory is just an echo
Let's just lie here and look up at the stars
Do your best not to think at all
Can you feel yourself moving?
You're moving all the time
Passing through at the speed of time
—◊—

Freedom
Isolating, freezing, total
Falling in every direction at once
You don't belong anywhere

No place has possession over you
You hold yourself prisoner
As protection
Like the inmate that calls the pig to lock him in
Security
Free to lose all freedom
Too much thinking involved
Reality becomes an enemy
Freedom, the huge night colored vacuum
So cold
—◦—

My killer
I walk to the mail box late at night
3 gunshots sound behind
I step into the shadows trying to do the invisible man
I see a figure running up the street
When I can no longer see him I come out and keep walking
If I didn't mail these postcards
I would be accused of being a stuck up rock star faggot
And we couldn't have that
Better to risk Death
Better to get a glimpse of my killer
My killer, my LA man
I never now when I'll run into him
It's going to suck
My killer will have no passion for his work
He'll waste me and think nothing of it
The detachment is so thick you would need...
Hell I don't know
A 16 year old will cut me down to impress his brother
Hello killer, see you soon
—◦—

Breathe in this hard luck perfume
The bars are full tonight
I walk down Sunset Blvd
Laid back loneliness
This place fills me with dirt and emptiness
I try to get a thought from the air
All I get is tarnished and devaluated
I never feel more alone than when I'm on the streets
On these busses, in their arms
I've never been to a place like this
—◦—

Can you walk through the streets and keep your head
Can you escape the poison cancer minds that bark and shriek
That welcome, love and fuck you?
Can you see them as enemy stranded?
Looking for a rat that's not drowning
Looking to introduce, infiltrate ingratiate and drain
Can you discriminate
Can you see and feel their disease
Do you understand the danger of a killer who works without passion
The one who learned detachment in the womb
Can you survey the decadence without apathy
Can you deal with the confusion coming at you with a crooked eye
Can you put litter in its place
Can you resist the downward pull of the modern noise?
Do you fully understand your role as a modern contemporary
Can you recognize the new model street warrior business man?
Can you see the meat for sale
Can you distance yourself from it all
Can you remember your name after a day full of this?
After a few lives full?
Will you be able to keep it up
Do you understand the new meaning of stamina
It's different than when your parents were young
More efficient automatic and deadly
Pity our flesh
It hasn't advanced as fast as the decadence around us

Could you touch me?
Fool me
Make me think that you like me
Could you do that?
I'd be willing to pay

Outside:
4 gunshots
A scream
Some one yells: Run, run
Then silence
No pigs
Nothing

Across the school yard down the street from my house

A female night scream:
Oh god, oh my god
I wonder is she's partying down or getting raped
Watching someone get stabbed or skinned alive

The man across the street empties his gun
Sends man made shooting stars into the sky
Everything gets quiet
The night creeps into my pores

100 plus homeboys fill the parking lot
Of a Hollywood mortuary
Someone got wasted
To see these guys
Dressed down
Cool and steel eyed
You figure even their DNA is mean

The sirens pass going east on Sunset Blvd
All the dogs sound off
Sad songs

I tell you, you're wrong
I did reach out to you
But my arms were too short
I called out to you but my voice didn't carry
You told me that I was insensitive, unfeeling, uncaring
Your eyes filled me with wordlessness
The closer I tried to get
The more I became trapped in myself
I wish I knew how to ask for help
I wish I knew how to talk
Then I could make you understand
Tonight I'm alone in my wasted planet room
Walking through the wreckage of myself
I was thinking that if you could see me
You would know what to do
I don't think I'm desperate
But I think that the blood of all these nights is filling my shoes
Maybe you could say something that would make us both laugh
Maybe you could teach me something about myself
I don't know if I'm telling the truth or if I'm lying all the time

I wonder if the truth would kill me right now
I reach for the phone to call you
My arm is too short again
I wish I knew how to ask for help

—⸙

Phone call:
She writes to make sense of it all
She has a filthified point of view
Last night she drank and punched holes in the wall
She pan handled for food money and bought some rice
She fights with her mother
She says her room is alive with roaches
She doesn't kill them because she hates the landlord
Insanity is the best way to communicate your deepest felt truths
This is a nasty stretch of land
A bad place to get shot in
Easy to get lost
Something to drink about
LA, the coveted Death machine
Amazing to see what we'll put up with and protect

—⸙

Walked the streets tonight searching my memory for you
Severe face, left nipple slightly exposed
You told me that you didn't trust yourself around me
The crime lights beat down on my thoughts
Another fool out on a Saturday night
Mortal, deformed by 1000 cities
Easy to walk and kick myself in the balls at the same time

—⸙

The stranger knows you, he sees you strange
He comes from a strange place
He locates you
He knows what you went through
Talk to the stranger
Touch the stranger
Marry the stranger
Kill the stranger
The one in your bed
The one on the bus
So what that it has a name
Anyone can name themselves
What do you understand

What did you ever understand
Blinded and brainwashed by orgasm
Now you're a stranger too
That's all you get
Talking in code and calling it something else
I call it a lie
That's why I stay on the outside
I'm tired of the codes
I'd rather take my chances in the outland
Outnumbered outmanned outlawed, fuck it
I know you very well, it breaks my heart
I see you clearly, it's truly ugly
The saddest song I've ever heard

When the dogmouths start to speak
I become a one man rejection society
This guy telling me about the next life
What, I have to do all this shit again?
The next life, the next lie
This one is enough
I get starvation first class
Weeks of the shit
I like it, it tells me what I am
Long periods of time when no one touches me
I become starved for touch and things get clear
I stare at women and they don't like it
Especially on trains
Where the hell are they going to go
I feel bad about it
I don't know if I would want
Someone to look at me like I'm their next meal
The ones with boyfriends bum out the worst
They can read the violence in my eyes
The hunger feels good
It's something to hold onto
Sometimes I like the pain that loneliness brings so much
I avoid contact with women
Like I've got this great roll going
And don't the pain to end

No one had touched me for weeks
I was starving

I met you in the middle of nowhere
I think of my hands on your body and I stop breathing
I remember melting into you
Everything was perfect
I am thinking of you through this bladed night
That doesn't have the guts to take me out
Will I ever see you again?
If I do will it matter?
There's only one road
One night at a time, one time at a time
Life has a way destroying you
Takes you out of the picture little by little
Ghosts you, fades you
Tracks you down and makes you speechless
Talking too much
I can't get you out of my mind

Tonight she's drinking
Calling everyone she knows and telling them the same stories
Tonight she's crying, her soul is full of bitterness
Life has become a huge and confusing weight
She tells him that she hates him
She tells him that he is the reason she wants to die
Quietly he listens patiently
Patiently he listens quietly
He listens he stays on the line
He stays on the line and listens
He listens
Tonight she's bumping into things
A glass crashes behind her as she goes to the bathroom
She sits on the toilet and cries into a handful of kleenex
It's the loneliest sound in the world
It comes through the walls
A tiny sad light in the middle of nowhere
She's so alone
She's not handling it well tonight
If only there was someone with her tonight
You should see the house
Everything is rusted, sprained, low on batteries and cold
10 days from now she will shoot herself

She walks by me

I smell her perfume
Beauty radiates from her like sunbeams
—

I study her face as she works
I am the Alien
All my nerves scream
On the outside I am calm, invisible
She has no idea what she does to me
To tell her would be a selfish display
I pay my money and walk out
—

Alien walk
The possibilities are endless
All things can happen to the One
—

How many nights I destroyed myself alone in a room
In the middle of nowhere, thinking about you
I told you how I felt and you shoved it into my guts
Then you didn't have to do it anymore
I learned to do it to myself
Why did the truth become my enemy
It was as if you had put a curse on me
You wouldn't let me get close to you
You rejected me and watched without expression
As I cut myself to pieces
I think of it as a lesson learned
You taught me a good one
I learned that none of you are worth it
What a fool I was to think that I could identify
All the time I spent thinking about you
Feeling that there was something wrong with me
Momentarily trying to avoid the truth
That's when the truth became my enemy
When I refused to see it, that's when it cut me
I think it was trying to wake me up
I still think of you but it's different now
To me you're all the same
I don't allow myself the luxury of having you mean much
I try to avoid the luxury of lies
—

Every moment that passes
My vision becomes sharper

With every breath I define myself more clearly
I become stronger
Remember that, I will always be strong
I will not go out like they did
With every rising sun
I eliminate untruths and poison from my mind
Everything benefits me
If I'm still alive then it benefited me
My scars are my teachers
Laces of strength
New eyes on my flesh
I will never win or lose
I'm not going to die
I'm going to get killed
—

The last American song
Over and over
Broken glass litters the street
Two in the morning
3 guys in a car buy it
His teeth are on the dash board
He can't feel his legs
He passes out for the second time
The paramedic puts the i.v. through the window
His two friends stand outside the car in shock
One tries to talk to the pig but can't find his mouth
Only then does someone notice his jaw is broken
He looks at the car and tells the pig:
My friend is drunk, I think he's fucked up
Mutilated puppets
Friday night entertainment
Los Angeles is a contest
A wrestling match
The night birds sing like sirens
Three in the morning
It's dead quiet in my hood
Then 4 shots followed by 2 return shots
The all's quiet again
It's 1989
I wonder how long until the magic runs out
—

Albert Ayler

Either you love him or hate him
His music either peers into your soul
Or sends you out of the room
I like him, he makes you choose
Of course there's none of that now
All the evil geniuses have been forgotten or destroyed
No music in these beautiful ruins
There is quiet
Then from out of nowhere comes an insane shriek
Like a ghost having a nervous breakdown
The spirits rise and shudder
Makes me think of Vietnam
All the bodies coming upwards through the mud and ash
An entire city's population emptying into the street
And having a mass epileptic fit
—◦—

Pull yourself up from the street
See them for what they really are
When I see them I want to see their shit burn
I want to tear the smiles off their faces
Listen to the shit that comes out of their mouths
You have to smile and be polite
When you should be putting them out of your misery
—◦—

Lock and load
Late at night I play Black Sabbath records
Makes perfect sense to me
When they say burn
When they say that the world sucks and that no one knows you
I know they are right
—◦—

Sat on the front porch tonight
Watched LA glitter and bleed
I thought of lost people
They took him in and sold him out
Inhaled him and blew him out
Lost a life at the bus stop
Turned his pockets inside out and found himself: empty
A single gunshot snapped me out of my thoughts
It came from across the street
Maybe he shot her
Maybe she shot him

Maybe someone shot themselves
What do you do when you get your shot
If all you had was one shot
What would you do
—•

He walks the streets like someone famous might have
Dirt clings to his soul
He is the botched abortion
The curse on the mother's lips
He is what happens
You can't surf around here but you can ride and ride
The walls are multicolored
A sprawling shelter
A glittering minefield
He walks thoughtless, less for them to take
Home is where the hate is
National Geographic would have a field day down here
Two girls, retarded
Gifts to the street
Drunk, hair pulling and saying bitch a lot
Crime lights are made for this
I'm going to do you a favor
I know you won't see it as such
I'm going to destroy your world
It's weak and filthy and needs to be put to sleep
It shouldn't take much
—•

It's 1:30 in the morning
The night is crawling up my spine
I'm going to call you on the phone
See if you want to come over here and fuck me
Like you did last summer
Maybe I won't call you
Maybe I'll sit here and breakdown in one of my ghettos
—•

The more you...
The more she'll...
If you ever...
She will first
Better
More completely
More vehemently

Than you ever thought possible
—◆—

To you
You who inspires me to seek out the emptiness of your smile
You have shown me the ghetto
You have shown me the ugliness
I have spoken to your back
I have caught your eye in passing
Your beauty gives me bad dreams
This is a bad night to be alive
—◆—

Pull a good fast one
Disappear in the face of adulation
Right when they're about to destroy you with praise
Right when they're going to define you and throw you away
Right before life becomes tragedy with a smile
Walk away
Remain
Don't fall for it
Don't fall
Once they got you, they got you
They'll wreck your life
They'll waste you
Walk away from ruin
Before you become ruin
—◆—

Alienated turned alienator
Alienator turned alienated
The child of dislocation
I grow distance in a rock garden
Alien turned cold animal in a distant hotel room
Turn off to turn off
Turned off by turn-ons
Turned away from everything that's warm
Warmth lies until it gets kicked out
Then it grows strong and cold
Or it dies
Facts are cold
The facts are in my distant hotel room life
Cold animal turned machine drill
Thought generator
Sometimes lies are necessary to deal with liars

Life leaves no clues
Life forgets me but will not let me forget
Holds me down and tells me that I'm free
I crawl from piece to piece
The ceiling has understanding eyes
Stares me down
While I make gestures in this still and silent life
—◦—

Last night I touched you
Tonight I don't know you
I can't stop the blood
Roaring in my ears, staining my sight
Shifting strangers walking point through jails and ghettos
They can't stop the blood
Moving down the hallways of brutality
Slaughterhouse circus antiseptic-minded
Numbed and partially destroyed
They can't stop the blood
Highway patrolmen holding handkerchiefs to their faces
As they look at the dead body they found
The pigs can't even stop the blood
Damaged from the start
Jaded before the first breath, burned out in minutes
Later dragged down, foaming at the mouth
Handcuffed and beaten beyond human limits
The blood seeps through the cracks, through tv screens
Through love and hate dreams
Last night I knew you
Tonight I destroy you and your memory
I can't stop the blood
—◦—

Koln
So I'm an animal
I'll fuck you and leave you
Fight you and not ask your name
I saw it in your eyes tonight
All your eyeballs
I know you know
Don't talk to me
I got nothing for you
Don't come near me
—◦—

Belgium
In this room I pull back and check the distance
It's all echoes and unknowns
Throttling time
Smashing memories to pieces
Rendering them powerless
I identify with the number One
I keep it with me at all times
—◦—

Without me this headache is nothing
It needs me more than I need it
It clings to me desperately
—◦—

Walked east on Sunset down the line of crime lights
Everything was bathed in pollution Death pink
Naked and burning
Through the haze downtown looked like it was burning
3 in the morning I'm walking east
What the fuck am I doing
Looking to get shot?
I walk until I see a pig chopper chase a car
I take my shirt off and let the air pass over me
No sound except the birds
Then a Pig chopper breaks it up
I live in Los Angeles
—◦—

Performing
We are good performers
Good onstage
Good thing we're good
We can't seem to get ourselves off the damn thing
Like when you're involved in the relationship
How much of it is the real thing
How much is it tapes from the last time around?
Something you heard on television
Do you know when you're being real and when you're acting?
It's something to think about
Did you give them a good one?
A good show
What happens when you fall off
You find yourself with yourself and you freak out
We love each other steeped in lies

When does it end?
Sometimes the mask slips and falls off
We see each other's real faces
Do you ever got the urge to get real and feel more lost than ever?
When you're alone and lonely
Do you want someone to be with
Or just someone in the audience to see the next show?

At the end I bet we're going to be on the front porch
Scratching our heads
Saying: We shoulda let'er rip!
Life I mean
You look around Silverlake CA
Damn
You see how low it can go in some parts
The nights are cheap and they bleed tired dirt
Dried loser's blood, bones and bullet casings
Sirens, helicopters broken safety glass
I hate to complain, but it all leaves me so cold
Gunshots don't make me flinch anymore
In 30 years everything will taste like tin
And we'll be used to it

I go through these women like they're nothing
I want it to be more than that
I want a woman that will drive me to distraction
A woman I can be wild about
It happened once
Only once and it's over with
Now it's a way to pass the time
No different than watching tv

It's nothing but the truth
These critics, these hounds of truth
Stupid as police
The woman sleeping next to me
I can't translate the heartbreak
It's cold and huge
Some thoughts must stay inside
When you let them out they get killed
They get hit by cars
They wander lonely and lost

They get taken by smiling con men
They can't stand up because they have no allies
No friends on the outside, that's how it is

I've been gone a long time
So long that I forgot I had a face
Forgot that I had a voice that you could hear
When you tell me how much I mean to you
And you want to know how I feel
I see my silence spit in your face
I didn't mean to throw a rock into your reflection
Maybe some things are better left broken and scattered
Veiled in darkness, secret bitterness and self doubt
I should have known better
Than to start something that I couldn't finish
That I couldn't care about
That I couldn't remember starting in the first place
I don't want to know you
You went years without me
You might as well keep going

Take a look around
Look at them
The one selling poison
One shooting the other
One ripping the other off
This is humanity
No
I cannot take the bad with the good
I don't see the separation so clearly any more
If this is humanity I'm climbing for higher ground
My ascension is in thought
My thoughts are directives to action

Decadence appeals only to assholes

Don't act with re-action
Re-act with action

Swimming in a lake of emptiness
Walking on the dark road
Staring out the window

Monitoring the train wreck in my head
Insomnia
10 years of dead cities
Barking
Echoes clapping
Waiting to be blessed with sleep
Staring at the wall
Feeling the strings attached to the backs of my eyes
Aching stones
I try to put on paper the ship wrecked starvation
That I feel inside
Have you ever spent an entire day amongst them
And not been able to figure yourself into any of it?
Ride on a train
Wonder if you exist
Watch the grey rush by
Try to find a thought that ignites you
In the eyes of your reflection
Ride a lifelong train
Tread water while you sit
Isolation
Not knowing what to do with yourself
Your stupid tool hands
That heavy face trying to slide off your head
If someone were to come into your room right now
And wrap around you
You would still think you were alone
And you would be right

Check in on the night shift
Calling all thoughts!
Fill up this vacancy
Nullify this paranoia
Clarify the monster thought
Give it all the weapons it will need
So it can try to rip me to shreds
Hard to find yourself as the end-up story
Looking at yourself
Seeing something that started and ended
Completion
Is terrifying

Women
It's sad that it's funny
It's hard not to laugh
It's hard not to cry
The same thing that makes men strong
Is the same thing that shoots them in the knees
Makes them turn on each other
Makes them into endless violent accidents
Baby
It's you
—◦

He looked at her all evening
Watched her mouth as she spoke
Watched the fabric of her pants
Define her raw perfection
Her beauty was staggering
It brought the room tight around his throat
Made him want to start fights
Or a war
That night he had dreams about her
The next day he saw that he was alone
He laughed like a dog
That got run over
—◦

You're spoiled
Selfish
Cruel through calculated ignorance
Beautiful
Then men will do circus moves at your feet
For a while
—◦

Tonight the entire room stands on my head
I am not the battle
I am the battle field
Brain wiped clean
Shot through with disinfectants
My will stripped to a brittle wire
I look at the phone thinking about calling out there
There's no one to call
Just voices
Other worlds
Sometimes I feel so thrown down

So used up and vacant
That I have to let time pass me by
—◦—

An outsider can laugh at them all
The alien walking outside the wire can look at them
Their torture sessions
And laugh at their bitter tears
Like the guy in the room
Not knowing how to deal with it
Unable to get her out of his mind
He hates himself because he can't stop it
He can't stop seeing her mouth and its smile
He feels stranded and used
He sees himself sitting in a chair
In the middle of a desert
His thoughts throw him into new ghettos
To avenues of ruin that he never knew existed
Yea, well it goes down all the time
The Alien walks the night trail
Looking through the man's thoughts
I laugh at you all the time
I am from your lost thought collection
When you go all the way out of yourself
You're with me
Look at the broken and the stranded
The road is littered with them
Pathetic wastes of energy
Mutilated pieces of human performance art
Years of denial for nothing
—◦—

I smashed out the windows of my room
No more natural light
Night time all the time
I am tired of the voices
The faces
The act
The windows of my room are broken
My world smiles now that you're gone
—◦—

I got your letter
I'm glad about the gun you bought
It's not unusual as the city story unfurls

As it crumbles
As the filth takes over
As humanity shits down its own throat
You will see that it was all just a play
A sketch
A mock battle
The mortal thrust
Equal to the garbage swirling at your feet
You're beautiful but not unscarred
A marred gem
The diamonds scratching the windows of poverty
Won't touch you
I'm glad about the gun
We could trade tales of ruin
We are the lucky ones
We get to see the world fall apart

How will I survive myself
I have headaches
I have shut every door
I see everything one way
All my thoughts are inbred
My teeth grind
I am violent
I am too late
I distance myself from people
So what
I won't survive myself
I will destroy myself with purpose
Animal with a brain
I need an on-off switch
A way to deaden the life that pounds through me
I have fantasies
The one where I walk out into the desert for days.
When I am far away from anything that is alive
I blow my brains out.
The one where I rip the spine out of a living woman
The one where I cut my vocal chords and ruin my face
The one where I sit right here
Until I die watching time
Torturing it by taunting its power
So destroy this night

Rage this existence
Push it over
Bring it to a boil
Rip the muscle off my bones
Inject exhaustion and insanity into my veins

Here we are
We can still do this
Burn without burning out
See with the unflinching eye
Take power to find new power
Walk alone where it's cold and dark
Maintain
Not burden others with our weakness
And call it something else
Do you feel it?
Your legs growing tired
The load becoming heavier
Yes it's all happening right now
The turn on
The high high
I want to see how you handle it
I want to see you deal with high velocity life
I want to see big sparks fly from you
Yes you

You light my head on fire
You make life thick and unbearable
I would rather think of 1000 nails pounded into my skull
Than you
You turn me into the definition of ignorance
Too much beauty at once
You show me how small I am
I turn into a self reduction machine
Something about expectation
Selfishly trapping you with my mind
Taking myself out and thinking that you did it to me
Please come here and do something to me
Anything

I am looking at a picture of myself
In the picture I'm smiling

I know better than that
I wear a mask
On the outside that's what they see
I don't want to talk about the rest of it
I don't want them to ask about me
I don't want them to know me
I put a magnifying glass on myself
I dissect, I look closely, too closely
I fall silently into myself
Self perpetuated, self involved, self destroyed
I don't want for interaction with others
That kind of perspective is not true
It's true to life, not true to me
Time to go outside
Where's the mask

Tonight turns the hands into fists
Shoves them deep into my pockets
Sends me out to the streets to walk
Sends my brain into rewind
Forces my head under one more time
I can't believe that I haven't drowned in my sea already
Always ready to take one more selfless plunge
Imagine diving into a pool of broken glass
A girl once said to me:
What's your problem, it sounds like you got burned once
I told her that I'm just burning
What the fuck does she know about me
Shove the world up your ass tonight
No one knows you
Don't let them tell you what your life is about
I tell myself this as I walk
Still I find myself listening to them
Trying to understand myself through them
Tonight attaches a leech to every blood cell that I possess
Punches me in the face with the past
Opens new wounds
Dissolves scar tissue
Sends me further into myself
Deeper than I thought I could go
Over and out

Look inside the wound
What do you see
The many headed night
The endless ever shifting possibility
Rip away the covering
See what you're made of
See the damage done, it's all you
Crawl inside the wound
Something wonderful is going to happen
Something terrible
Wrap the wound around you
Become the wound
Choose it before it chooses you
See motherfathermonster
Cocksuckerviolentbloodhatebreeder
Inhale
It slams you
Sizes you up and magnifies all the bad stuff
The truth
Live the wound
Wounded in the womb
Pounded into the tomb
Walk the perimeter of the wound
It's that Abyss that looks through you all your life
Find shelter in the wound
Get away from them
They'll never understand you
They're too busy with their wounds
No matter what you think
They only get a glimpse
Some more than others
—

I want a woman to kill me
I want to be stopped
I want to be destroyed
I want to be shot in the head by a woman
I saw her tonight in the store
I knew she was the one
She saw me looking at her
I followed her into the parking lot
Hoping she would pull out a gun
And end this pain

feel vacant and shattered
.e understands
I w.../find the right woman
She will help me
She will kill me
She will stop this pain
It gets worse everyday
All I want to do is get out
I want a beautiful woman to kill me

Beautiful

I can't forget you
You kissed me I nearly started crying
I wanted to die right at that second
You touched me and then you walked away
You made me feel alive
I can't stop thinking about you
I want to kill someone
I want to kill all the time
I walk the streets following people
Thinking of all the ways I could do it
I can't contain my rage
Words can't describe what I feel for you
They don't do justice
The only thing I can do is kill people for you
To take life and destroy it
I put myself to sleep by punching holes in the wall
I love you

Gone too far to be forgiven
Can't undo what I've done
Can't repair what or whom I broke
Gone too far to change
People don't change
They find better ways to cover themselves
Gone too far to take the lines from my face
Can't not see what I saw
This is it
There's a long trail behind me
A shorter piece up ahead
The brightest lights have shone
The loudest roar has been uttered

And now I'm getting down to it
Instances of time flash and pass
They get suspiciously similar
I see the same things
With different names in different places
Gone too far to ever love your world
Know too much to ever call it home
Gone too far to not see the fist in my hand
Know enough to know that I'll always come crawling back
To learn the same lessons in pain
I've gone too far

Don't let the despair crush you
When it comes crashing in it wrecks you
Smash Ugly Tragic Destroyed
Can't handle the nights sometimes
I take it one breath at a time
Can't talk to anyone
The despair comes to you like a disease
Don't let it control you like it controls me
You can tell by looking at my eyes
The only thing stopping me...
I fear prison
I don't fit into this world
I don't like to look at women
For hours at a time all I can think about
Hurting myself and others
Anything that can feel
Anything that can register pain
I am lonely and I want to see it in someone else's eyes
The gunshots outside tell me
Others have reached their limit
Everyone has their own way of dealing with it
Don't let despair mutate your flesh
Look at my twisted stumps of thought
See the fingers, listen to the voice
I am slowly becoming the end of the line

Paranoia climate
Nice out tonight, wind in the palm trees
I can smell the ocean from here
A car with tinted windows slowly passes

Everything tells me to
Run hide duck dive lock load attack
And there's you
You're beautiful tonight
Infinite and full of possibility
What do you want from me
How many way do you know how to hurt me
Where's your knife
I don't believe your smile
Maybe you want to kill me
Maybe you want to use me
What do you see in me
What are you looking for
I don't know if I should let you do
Or if I should do to you first
I know me but I don't know you
This night is real
The Crips hanging out down the street
The crack headed woman picking her face
The neighbors pitbull foaming away
Beautiful
But not as beautiful as you
—◦

I know you find me easy to forget
I think of you endlessly
Your tortured streets
How they glitter and wound
Your late calls to tell me nothing
Dreams of you leave me weak
The night is a leech
Your gunshot eyes
You're laughing somewhere right now I bet
Twisting some idiot in knots
You empty pockets dreams and gas tanks
Take the taste right from the mouth and trash it
Make the fool think that everything he feels is wrong
I'm in my cell thinking that I sidestepped you
I'm wrong
You would throw me away in the blink of a glass eye
What's the use in talking to you
You already know what I'm thinking
This room is empty
—◦

The night is alive with gunshots
Where are wounded tonight
You know the feeling
You've seen the invisible clawmarks rise
Your thoughts have been run over in traffic
I am thinking about thoughtlessness
I don't want to think of you anymore tonight
The impossibility of you and me is hard to take
Truth can break your arms while you sleep
I wonder if your beauty wounds you as it does me
Where are the wounded tonight
If I didn't find myself, everything would be alright
But I always do find myself
Ugly and cheap
A freaked out violent human mess
I am sure your touch heals wounds
Someone else's
A cannon blast outside
I think of blood, brains, your face, the moon
End this pain

I carry a faded picture of you in my head
Your smile is barely visible
Part of it got lost in a human loss joke
On a train
Or maybe in one of those instances where it seems
Like existence is trying to hammer you into a crust
I don't think like I used to
But I still think of you sometimes
Just to see what will happen
Used to make me leap
Now it's just a flicker
The picture keeps fading
As I walk farther into the desert
Of violence, paranoia and isolation

I'm better off here in my room
When I see them
Smell them
Hear them
I want to kill them
Shoot them

Burn them
Make them kill each other
Light each other on fire
Rape and imprison each other
More than they do already
I got Black Sabbath turned up loud
I'm trying to beat my thoughts to Death
I need more power, more volume
Violence on an epic level
So I can sleep without dreams
I look at them in magazines
Smiling through garbage eyes
I want to shove the world up their ass
Make the police fist fuck each other on MTV
I got Jimi Hendrix turned up to Vietnam velocity
Outside their world is burning
Inside I am laughing always

Always knowing you're going to die
And until then knowing you've got to live

So leave me to the black hours
I will watch the air shift
You're right, let's not waste time
Don't talk, just leave
Alone makes sense
It's all I know
The rest of the time I'm faking it
Doing television outside of the glass eye

Isolation fell away
I found myself here
Same place
I'm not isolated from anything
I'm here by choice
All is clear to me
I am a brother to biology
I am alone

Berlin Germany:
A woman with a see through blouse walks by me
I look at her breasts

She looks at me scared and offended
Another woman walks past me
Her skirt is short
She keeps pulling it down to conceal her panties
I stare at her as she yanks the tight cloth
She holds her skirt down and walks away glaring
What the fuck do you expect to happen
What do you think you have between your legs
Secret treasure
You make me laugh

So what happens to you when the dreams have been destroyed?
When you have chased cornered and ripped them limb from limb?
When you walk away to a desert inside yourself
I fell into the vacuum of my room
The darkness tortured me
Sucked the air through the cracks in the floor
Time scars my thoughts
I have thought about calling or writing one of you
Trying to reach out and touch one of you
I never get to it
I can't get out of myself
I couldn't find the right words to show you where I am
It used to be terrifying
Talking myself out of shooting myself in the head
Now it's just conversation
The night brings the silence and lies
With which keep myself alive
I hold myself in fragile arms
I'm not strong
I'm a rat holding on one handed to the screen of the drain

Electric coffee night
Black and unfolding
Full of promise
The lie that life provides
Keeps me cutting myself
Keeps me drawing darker blood
My brain is getting the fat trimmed
I'm breaking smiles on the street
Breaking bones, breaking light
Insanity fills this small hot space

I don't read character into it
Carbon monoxide has choked the pollution from my thoughts
I wait like a human for the last shove
—◦-

I only care about living- ask anyone
I don't care about dying- don't tell anyone
—◦-

I'm sick of cities
Dirt rising off the streets
The air red with maniac words
I am sick of not cities
Quiet undisturbed crippling landscape
I need weakness to feel strong
Perspective of the impatient loser
I'm sick of in between cities
Motion sickness keeps me hanging on
Swinging by Death's eyes
I'm sick of stagnant time
My blind, raged, weak life has swallowed me whole
I am sick of myself
—◦-

New Zealand Hotel Jet Lag Blues
Don't want you to follow me
Don't want anyone to follow me
Into the wound
This room is dark
Spinning
You can watch
You can touch
But you can't come
The world doesn't care
It chews and spits
I walk alone into the wound
All the darkness
Madness and ruin
—◦-

After I had finished playing I stank
My sweat had turned to ammonia
I was sitting alone watching it form puddles at my feet
This girl came and said hello
She asked to feel my gluteus maximus
I stood up in ignorance

I figured if she was going to kick me in the balls
I would stand a better chance if I could move
She put her hand on my ass
She said it was nice like Fred Astaire's
She said that she was a psych student
She had watched us play and had analyzed it
She thought I was abusive when I punched that guy
She thought the rest was infantile
She looked nice
I was going to ask her if she wanted to fuck
I figured she would understand such an infantile approach
A guy walked up to us and nervously stated that he liked the show
He looked at her and told her it was time to leave
I stood her up and moved her to the guy
They looked a little scared then
They left quickly and that's good
The only thing that made sense to me right then
Was to mutilate the guy and ask her if she wanted to fuck
Spindly motherfucker walking away with the bitch
When I could kill him
This cage is too small
These examples of civilization shouldn't get so close

I've see it happen so I know this for a fact
They will throw themselves at your feet
Lie and belittle themselves
To seem large enough to impress you
Waste time and lose sleep
Spend money like it's nothing
Transform themselves
Into vile human superhero shit heads
Hoping to make you smile
The rest is up to you
If one doesn't please, another one will come soon
To flagellate himself for your viewing pleasure
You can destroy them with a smile
Your touch can make them hot blooded idiots
When that gets boring
You can play them against each other
Make them hate blindly
So you can laugh
At their seeming stupidity

It was easy to figure men out
A few mistakes at first
But now it's together
I played that shit game for awhile
I didn't mind
I knew it was a game
Some of these poor bastards think it's real life
And let themselves get taken to the cleaners
You see what happens
Heartbroken damaged wrecks in human suits
And you see what happens to you
Broken jaws and black eyes
Decomposing bodies discovered by hunters
And all the other women who do not share
Your terrifying traits
And instead are real people
Have to take the rap for you
They will always be around
Risking Death and humiliation
I am not one of them

A milk truck ran into a light pole on the corner near my apartment
I was 8
Scared of my mother's boyfriends
Skinny freaked out scabbed wild eyed and full of shit
The driver's head went through the windshield
Exploded on the light pole
Never occurred to me
The beauty of that
Blood brains and all that milk
It all ran down the gutter
I ran down the hill chasing the greying milk snake
To new fields of terror

Death
I've been looking for you
I have choked life
Shook it by its skinny neck
Fucked the taste out of its mouth
Made it scream
Made it want to die
Now I'm walking alone on the cinder trail

Come on
Show me something
—◦—

On the train to Trenton NJ
Hot
I can smell myself
The floor is covered with garbage
I see a girl on the platform
I wish I could lift myself from this and touch her
I wish I didn't want to break your arm
Do you want to know me?
My pain would break your rib cage
I could love you
I wish I could stop running
—◦—

So fuck it
Keep destroying until it all falls apart
Take a look at a world that overloads and distorts
That filthifies and fictionalizes
Prolongs life in order to torture and infect
Pull back and rip your eyes out to see
I don't see any fucking soul
You want love?
Go talk to your mother
She's choking on it
I ride my overdriven headache until I'm ready to explode
Walk the streets trying to let the pieces fall to the bottom
I don't see any of the soul you're spitting on yourself for
Here it is:
Human until dead
So fuck it
Destroy
If you want to end it
End it
End me
Stop this trail of burning footsteps
End yourself
Find a method to rip the pain away
Find a way to see through the lie
Clear your camp
There's no fucking soul here
—◦—

In my shattered mind
I had an unshattered dream
You put your hands on my face
You told me of your deepest pain
You asked to take your pain away
Somehow I did
I don't know how
You asked if you could do the same for me
I told you that you already did
I'm glad it was only a dream
I need my pain
I want my pain with me always
Dragging me down the cinder trail

Don't take this ruptured body man to your home
Don't embrace him
Don't try to warm him with your kindness
Your every gesture will be rejected
This world overwhelms and terrifies him
He can't cut it
He is unable to translate his rage
He can't touch you and feel it
He can't hear your voice
His thoughts lay scattered at his feet
Swirling
They are made of ash

Once the wheels start to roll
And the guts of the machine roar to life
I forget you
Thoughts of you are crushed to a fine powder

I'm glad you don't respond to me
Days are passing
I'm forgetting you
I'm going on without you
It hurt for a lot longer than I thought it would
A lot longer than I was willing to admit
I get stronger as time passes
I move with time
We both forget you
The self inflicted wounds that spell your name

Are healed and gone
—•

Fuck it
Life is an embarrassment
Every breath threatens to pull your pants down
The lies are stacked in obscene piles
Makes me think of a dead man
Swinging in an apartment by an extension cord
The note in his pocket reads:
I stopped it, it did not stop me
I'm not going to grow old
I'm not in love with this heap
I will stop it
It will not stop me
Language falls out of my mouth
Ritual habit
Love hates
Truth lies
Blah blah blah
The convenient torture methods
Stacked layered and crammed in to every pore
Until you're forced to stand next to yourself
On bended knees
With all the smirking clown faces
Without motion and confrontation
Without my hand around life's throat squeezing
Forcing definition from this diseased confusion
Life is an insult
So fuck it
I'm taking it down the cinder trail
And I don't want to hear about
What you think you stand for
Because it's nothing
Furniture, boxes, bonfires, lists
A cast of renters
The embrace, the kiss, the long look
Falls to the floor on Death row
Life is an embarrassment
—•

It's 1991
We fuck at her boyfriend's house
—•

The sun is setting
I'm getting ready to meet my friends
Insomnia and Paranoia visit often
They will keep me up and at it for the next 12 hours
The night is young
Strong enough to keep me in this choke hold

The other night I was with a woman, I was awake and crying at 5:30 AM.
My silent shaking woke her up. She insisted that I explain myself. I tried
to tell her what I have never told anyone. What I try so much to forget.
The blank hours of silent horror. White shapes obscenely waving at me
from the corners of my eyes. The anguished sleep that follows after sun
up. My story came out as a few words, some moans and a lockjawed
silence. I cannot remember ever feeling farther away from the human
race. It's hard for me to not stop this pain forever, knowing what I know.

I have to keep moving
I don't want to think
I'm going to work all day today
I don't want to stop
Don't want to let my brain catch up my thoughts
How will I be able to tell them that I'm a shadow
A grey patch of cold rotting light

Some things are too embarrassing
I could never tell you
I could never tell anyone
How much I think about you
How it scares me
Every morning as insomnia's grip loosens
I stare at your picture
I think of your painful shyness
Your ravaged self opinion
Your incredible beauty
How drawn I am to you

The nights have not moved
It's been weeks since I've slept well
Usually it's the long vigil
I watch the sun come up
In total silence
Hours later I am with them
I can't identify

I don't have any idea
What the hell they're talking about
The hours pass and night moves in
Paranoia comes
Sinks its teeth in and holds on
I can see the scars

You are the reason I don't want to die all the time
When I am with you life is worth living
Time away from you is strange and full of pain
When I look into your eyes
I can see how life has savaged you
It's ok if you fall
I will be there to catch you
Anyone that would want to hurt you
Would have to kill me to do it
I will never be able to pound words into lines
To match the velocity of your presence

I wonder where you are
It's been weeks since I heard from you
All this time, nothing
I have lost sleep thinking about you
I wonder if you want me
I call your number
I Listen to your voice on the answering machine
Now I'm in this basement lifting weights
Making sure it hurts
I wish I could see you instead of looking at your picture
Feeling like an idiot
I try to remember what your hair feels like
It hurts
I don't know if you are being straight with me
Lies are hard to take
I am a fool

I will never let you know how much you hurt me
No, I will never tell you
The last few months have sent me into myself
It's not easy to forget you
Time is healing me
I keep my feelings to myself, it helps

I don't understand you or your kind
I end up getting myself messed up
I can't take anymore beatings like this
—

Too bad for me that I think of you
My arms want to fall off
I want to hold you
My arms remember you
They wonder what they have done to deserve this
They are starving
Me too
If you were here right now
I would show you something
—

In dead hours
Sitting in my room
Face in my right hand
Music playing
Thinking about him
His hands in your hair
The scent of your skin
Making his eyes close
Your breath on his neck
—

It was all in my mind
You were never there at all
I wanted you to be though
When you would smile at me
It made up for years of wounds
They didn't matter
Now I see that it was just me
Losing my mind again
—

As she becomes
Away
I watch myself try to hold onto her
I have never known a pain like this
—

You might say that I am over reacting
No one is worth all this
It couldn't have been that good
You're wrong
—

I can't kill myself yet
I have not finished my work
I must keep my presence of mind
I must work until I reach
One
—*

I thought I meant something to you
Obviously I was wrong
You should have told me
You should have kept me at a distance
—*

I've been thinking about you
Driving myself to distraction
You're so beautiful
I miss you so much
It's so hard to take it when you lie to me
When you touch me
Life is livable
It's worth sticking around
The pain and the paranoia go away for awhile
And then you lie and everything rots
—*

Today I drove through a ghetto in Trenton NJ
Garbage and who gives a fuck everywhere
Hard eyed black men staring bricks through my face
In the middle of this endless slap in the face
I saw a white house
Some historical landmark
The lawn was smooth green
Even the sky above seemed bluer
Surrounding the house was a high chain link fence
Topped with barbed wire
I imagined the maintenance men coming out every morning
To pull down the dead that got ensnared at the top
Like sharks on a net
—*

How many mute hours will I spend
Thinking of you
I count the days that I don't call you
To ask you not to leave me here so incredibly alone
As steps in the right direction
9 days now and I'm feeling alright

Soon I'll go back to my old ways
One night adult shuffles
But I'll always remember you

I wish I knew a woman I could be with
Who would touch and love me
A woman who was strong
So I could stop swallowing all this rage for awhile

I stare at the phone like it's a stupid animal
Silently it mocks me
I could call her and leave another pathetic message
Or worse, actually talk to her
Make a fool of myself again
While she listens without comment or emotion
She doesn't want me
I know this but I am so lonely
I miss her

The years of rage and bluster have thickened the blood
Pulled the cover away to reveal a ravaged man
Sickened by life
Who sees too deeply - too far - always

I was half listening when she said:
I have been faithful since I started going with him
8 months ago
Me not so desperately trying to remember her name
As I checked out her scars from breast implant surgery
She was fine and we faked it all night
On some other girl's couch
Weeks ago I wouldn't have bothered with this shit
But now I am back to my Death trip
And I feel fine

When you go insane there will be nothing
When you go insane there will be no one
Nothing to hold you
No one to love you
No one to talk to you
But it won't matter
It won't matter if the walls are grey

Or that time is hollow and lonely
And passes whistling and hissing like wind through high weeds
I'm laughing and shrugging all the way to Death
I've never known a moment of real life
Watch me as I run mindlessly and directionlessly
Forward

If I thought it would help
I would stay with you for as long as it took
I would show you something different
That I was telling you the truth the whole time
As it is right now
I have taken all I can
Your shallowness has thrown me into a deep hole
It would be better for me to hate you I know
But I can't
I try but I keep thinking of you sitting alone
Seeing yourself as pieces of broken glass on the floor
Your inverted rage is hard to be around
Good luck

My loneliness is so large that it has outgrown me
It walks beside me, a wasteland that keeps in step
Sometimes our shoulders touch
It feels like teeth sinking into my flesh
A new and strange stretch of desert opens before me

If you want to hurt them and their children not yet born
Tell them the truth always
When you meet them
Stare deep into their eyes
Take those who wish to dominate you
Turn the game around and play it on them
Don't spare them a thing
Make sure you tell them about the blood and the pain
They can say what they want
You will trigger all their responses
It's all blood and Death from here
You won't be kept waiting long

There's nothing better than a woman
There's nothing more evil than a woman

Living or dead

Don't think about killing yourself yet
You have not finished your work
Until you are finished you will have to take the pain
Don't think, just work
Do your writing
Tour without taking time out to relax
Don't think that you will meet a woman
This is bullshit just shut up and work
The way you have been carrying yourself lately has been disgusting
What the fuck has gotten into you?
Just work
Shut your mouth and work

Death will take me soon
I hear it in my room at night
Putting guns in my mouth
Turning the dark hours into eternities
I ask when
The dark face is expressionless and silent

He blew his brains out with her smile

I bet her touch heals
I imagine her apathy strangles
I know her absence kills

There was nothing I could do
To make her feel anything
Short of killing her
But even then
She'd just spit blood in my face
And walk away

I could shut down cities with the things I say
You know what I mean
These hotel rooms kill me slowly

Man with the writhing face
Nose hammered flat

Sleeps on a grate
Alcoholically numb and dead still living
Another body bag urinates on him
Death rocks on his heels
Warms his hands and hurries on
Toronto Saturday night
—+

I wanted to ask the whore
How she deals with the cowardice of men
I didn't do it
I didn't want to know that much
—+

How disgusting to watch these youths with their eyeliner and fucked up hair stand and beg for change. This crippled strength. Reduced to begging. Getting flattened and mutilated by life. Looking at them I get all the inspiration I need. Never relent. Never take your hand off of life's throat. Always pursue. Stalk. Life is nothing but a test.
—+

To take a step into this vast emptying desert
This lit up hope filled expanse
This space that reduces us to the truth
To embrace this life extinguishing process
To constantly fuck with Death
To live through this slaughter without killing yourself first
This is dot dot dot
—+

I don't want you
I want the vacuum
The Abyss
The Apocalypse
Death's slow smile and sound marching step
Have a good trip
—+

For me it's the ever widening shadows
A silence that steadily increases in volume
Separation from myself
So that I walk alongside my body
I hear their voices like wind in high grass
Darkness is rushing forward
—+

If I could I would melt into your arms
I would fall like 10 dead languages

I would not front
I would not lie to you
I don't think I could lie anymore
I have grown too old for such youthful pursuits
I want to love someone before I die
Hurry
It won't be long now
—❦—

He was a human being diseased with life
She was a city resident
He got too close
Hurt himself with his stupidity
Showed all of himself
She tore him apart
He retreated to the shadows
He is confused and wracked
Parts have been burned away
Some feelings will never come back
He no longer trusts his feelings
They hurt him before
He thinks about Death all the time
It's the only thing he knows that's coming
—❦—

She never loved a man in her life
She started hating her father
And took it from there
The ones she doesn't destroy
She wounds and inspires
They pull themselves out of the wreckage
After a few months they can walk again
—❦—

I can't maintain a relationship
I am too cruel and selfish
I don't know how to get out of myself
I might as well get on with it
Finish the work and then die
It's all I'm good for
The rest is bullshit
I'm looking forward to checking out
—❦—

All we do is eat sleep and worry about the rent
Somewhere there is real life

And those who live it
What about the rest
Paralyzed by television and police chokeholds
Alas
Life widens and grows distant
—◦—

I don't have a gun in my room
I wake up every night in this place
The only thing I can think of is shooting myself
I think about doing it in the garage
It would only take a second and then nothing
So now I'm up and letting it pass so I can try and sleep
In the morning I will try my best to deal with them
—◦—

Every morning I think of what I would say if you called
I have thought about it so many times
Even though I know I'll never see you again
I ask people if they've seen you
They say they haven't
A lot of people hate you
I don't know what you did
From what they say you have a history
One said:
You fuck them and then you fuck them over
I don't hate you
I wish I could have gotten to you before
All those men smoked your heart
And ground you out
—◦—

On the way to facelessness
I'm not going to lick the streets anymore
No more mistakes
There was a momentary hitch to my passing through life
Just a bend in the road
I think I tried too hard
—◦—

Burn the fat out of the tissue
I don't want to blunt the pain
I'm so tired of fucking around
I think that's why we live so long
The bullshit keeps us alive
If that's the case

Fuck this place

The loneliness that the world generates
We keep it going all night long
Waiting for a dull moment, or a lot of dull moments
To sneak away from the pain
During these unmoving silent nights I feel its crushing wheel
Is there anyone in the world that I can know?
I am tired of knowing myself so well

No drugs, no pain killers
Nothing to dull the pain
I want the Abyss
Straight no chaser
I want to see clearly
For once, for real
So what if it kills me
So what if it tears me to pieces

Could I talk to you and have you not run away?
Could I touch you and have it be alright?
Could we connect somehow?
Could we get rid of all the dead bodies
All the dead time
All the walls
All the shields that keep us standing?
Could you help me get rid of mine for a few hours?

I am the silent shell
Crashed out after a show
I watch the sweat run off me again
The silence is untranslatable
Farther away from them I go
On my way to casualtyville
I am harder than loneliness
I scare it, it leaves me alone

I will try my best to keep working
Until I finally burn myself out
The problem I have, it plagues me
No matter what I try to do
The depression wears me down

It's like chip encoded into my brain
I can keep it at bay for short periods
But it's stronger than I am
I will give it my best shot
It might take my brains with it
—◆—

I have killed another day
I didn't give it a good fight
I just shot it in the back
And watched 400 miles pass by
My blood stains the bedsheet
—◆—

Thoughts come
They halt and resign themselves to suicide
I mask total clarity with exhaustion
And tell the Abyss to leave a message
I'll get in touch when I get the chance
—◆—

I would like to lie next to you
Put my face on your neck
Feel your hand on my back
Hear the sound of your steady breathing
As you save me from the darkness
That will someday catch me alone and destroy me
—◆—

Small cracks in my frame
Caused by minor earthquake thoughts
I wonder if the waitress knows
That I shot her in the face
3 times already
—◆—

I work until exhaustion folds my edges
I do my best
I strive for dreamless sleep
A temporary coma to relax in
—◆—

When we're not killing each other
We kill ourselves step by step
There will always be someone
To help you
To fill your shoes with blood
To fill your mind with idle time killing time

Sometimes it's you

I can stack the blocks of emptiness
One on top of the other
(I build it night by night)
Soon I have a wall to hide behind
A place to go
After awhile I get used to it
Slowly paralyzed into submission
I float on the breezes of extinction
Please touch me

I can die any time I want
I wish I could do the same with life

Corpses don't get paranoid
Paranoia is for the clear and fragile minded
I've paid my dues and dulled myself
And nothing gets in my way

These people
The ocean of flesh that roars nightly
If they only knew
How fucked up the conductor is

If you want someone
You can have me
You don't have to be anyone but yourself
Maybe you can help me find myself
I'm blinded by noise and rage
I think I killed my better half
Somewhere back there

I mutilate myself nightly
I don't know what else to do
Maybe watch someone else?

Walking alongside life
Not daring to get in front or back
Finally
Walking the opposite direction

And not looking over my shoulder
—◦

I'm making the best of it
Working in the world of pain
Good boss
Never a question as to who's in charge
—◦

I'm so fucked up
I don't know if I'm lying
Or if I'm...
—◦

I need witnesses to my problems
I don't have the strength to deal with them alone
I need you to watch and listen
And approve
—◦

Pull down your wall tonight
I'll do the same
I promise I won't hurt you
I won't turn your honesty into humiliation
I only do that to myself
It pays the rent
See what I mean?
—◦

The night air is moist and unmoving
I can smell car exhaust as I walk
You have a voice no one will ever hear
I keep it close to me
—◦

I will do my best to dodge tonight's depression
Hide in sleep
Damage myself in dreams
Wake up older, slightly more used
In the present tense
In the present tension
—◦

I must be hard and smooth
Like the concrete floor underneath my feet
Flesh fails me, infuriates me
I must push past it as far as I can
I must stay close to the spare and lean

Only then can I respect myself
—

For a few hours
Let's forget life's uselessness
With my eyes closed I can trace your shape
I wish your hands were on me right now
—

The singer in the other band was drunk
He slurred his words
The crowd loved this pathetic insult
 "I drink because there's so many assholes"
I watched the pretty girls wave and scream
I was born too late
I should have been a Samurai
Aspiring to the sword and Death
These days people are withered
The spirit has been made to whine
They'll never get me
—

Livin' large:
Lots of shit is heavier than life
Like shooting a pig in the face
Like Vietnam
Homicide speaks louder than words
Suicide is more intense than
 I love you
Crime is the only thing man invented to justify life
San Quentin is more mystifying
Than all them thar triangles stickin' out of the sand in Egypt
—

I must finish the work
Untie all the knots
Straighten all the lines
Sharpen the blade
The will to complete keeps me alive
—

Boston night:
I walk the streets
There's certain things I can't say aloud
I want to give you diamond thoughts
Not cough up blood and coal
—

I Fling myself into the Abyss
All thoughts to the desert
Alas
I see clearly through hollow eyes
My real voice has no sound

It feels good to kill a mosquito
A female that sucks your blood
Smashed against a wall, legs broken

I am getting the body stronger
Expanding the pain threshold
Opening the eyes wider
Heading towards the roaring slaughter
I won't stand a chance

Do you ever silently wish
For the strength of someone else
Do you ever imagine what it would be like
To be touched for the first time in 100 years
Everything in me wants you and Death

The iron is my friend my hero
Detects my weakness
Shows me where to go
Strengthens my number
Never fails
The iron makes life worth living
Stabs self doubt
Mutilates depression
Opens gates of light
My body aspires to Iron

I have been reduced by force to this
All I do is restrain myself from killing you
I have seen the eyes of existence
There was blood in the corners
I did not run away
Civilization has crippled me
And that's lucky for you

I maim the body of life

Send it running scared
Never let it sleep
I rest my body so I can push it the next day
I'll scare the life right out of my bones
If I could I'd give myself my own funeral
Invite myself and do it
Murder life in its sleep
Snap its spine and take it with me

Death is my reference point
No matter how bad the shit can get
I'll never slap the smile off Death's face
Now that Death is my guardian and true north
Everything in me is stronger
My perspective is a tool
No longer a hindrance for my ego
What a high

On an airplane going to Frankfurt Germany
13 shows /13 days /6 countries
Taste the blade
Tight rope walk from stage to stage
Control the rage
Deal with the cage
Feel the age
Turn the page

Tried to find you with my eyes closed tonight
I got to your face and that's it
Something switched off
The impossibility of you and me
I can't remember how I felt then
It doesn't matter
You were a bag of lies and excuses
You let your life turn you into shit
You're like all the others
I must have been out of my fucking mind

Need is a disease
Makes you crawl
You'll end up hating yourself
And you'll need something else

To take the pain away
And then you'll need to forget it all
And then you'll need to get back on track
And then you'll be another 24 hour a day need freak
I needed to tell you this

Germany
My body is covered with road stench
Diesel, tobacco, sweat, grease and dirt
Men's room, rasthaus, no sleep
I don't want to wash it off
It's a second skin
Keeps my back straight
It insulates me from disease
Tonight I will sleep with it on

I'm sorry if I hurt your feelings
Believe me it's the last thing on my mind
Sometimes I can't control myself
I have nothing to say to you
When you talk to me I want to kill you
Just to keep you away
I'm not of your world
I gave you all I got
There's no more questions to ask me
No matter what
You never talk to me anyway
So let's leave it alone

I wonder how you're getting along
When you told you didn't want me anymore
There was no emotion in your voice
Part of me died
Everything slowed down
I still think about you before I go to sleep
I don't tell anyone how much it hurt me
I'm too damned embarrassed
And besides
All the talking in the world couldn't change a thing
I wish I never met you
You are something I regret
I wish it was over

It's never over

I knew she would show up
She always does
Tells me the same story
Her husband left her for her friend
She wants me
She tells me as she stares at me
I have been offstage for about 3 minutes
It is impossible not to hate her guts
I don't want anyone wanting me
It makes me sick

I don't want to know you
I have nothing for you
I don't even have a self for myself anymore
People pick at your body like crows
You want a friend, go hang out with a big rock
It's not me you want
No matter what you think

The road is a disease that bites your bones
Mostly it infects your mind
You think you're a mass of speeding electric velocity
You tell yourself that you're living
But you know you're just chasing shadows
Calling them spirits
I'm waiting for the dust to settle
For language to die
I want to breathe for the first time

I am immune
Too exhausted to notice
Too paranoid to sleep or wonder for too long
Too self abused and withdrawn to help myself
Real life doesn't come close to this

Welcome to this pure example of perfect human sadness
Your life in the finite ghetto
Yes your life is short
Yes your days are numbered
No you'll never escape

Touch the invisible wall of the ghetto
Man made
Run wild and get your wings singed
Find yourself in my arms
Your blood maniacally racing
Not even it can escape the ghetto

Love heals scars love left
We're all hypocrites
Searching desperately
Before our ability to attract
Takes too much effort to use
Or disappears much to our horror

We die trying to impress each other
I'd rather be respected by a bolt of lightning

I like my world
Right now it's all I can stand
Get too close and they'll take you to the bottom
They fuck me up
I go to the store and I have to listen
It's a non-stop tragedy
The night is here though
No gunshots
I wish the Sun would take a vacation
Leave me in darkness for awhile
Let me heal
Let try to figure out why I'm fucked up

He was prone to long battles with depression
He lost a long time before he won
But it wasn't for long
Depression would find him and tear into him
Drain him like a leech
Depression came to become the one constant in his life
He lost his armor and shields miles ago
Now everything goes right to the bone
He walks with Death in every step
He lives a secret life
No one ever sees him
He cannot find words for the rage inside

He sees a woman
She says she loves him
He says he loves her
He doesn't love anything
All he thinks about is Death
He spends the days in silence
Sometimes there's a call
He gets through it as fast as he can
There's no one he wants to talk to
He waits for the night
He listens to music in the darkness

Keep me from thinking about my parents
Keep the horror out of my mind
I wish I never met them
They bring me nothing but the coldest pain
Thinking of her weakens me
I don't know what to say to her
I feel like a stranger
I don't want to be part of their lives
But I am
It makes me want to die
All the time
The older I get the worse it gets
I don't know what to do
I wonder if there's anyone who never felt free
Until their parents were dead

They have no idea
Why I'm in this
For me it's all about rising to the occasion
Confrontation
Fuck it
Let's see the muscle pull away from the bone
Let's see some fucking pain
I want to see it when you're not so fucking cool
Ok, so it's just me out here
Fine
I'll show you

Life sees through you
Walk on a tightrope of vertebrae

10 years of spine
Take a photo
At this point it's an x-ray
Life passed through me
Left me here
I'm figuring out what to do
With the remaining time
—◦—

I'm obsessed with documentation
I must record every drop
I have good equipment
I don't miss much
It's a sickness
An obsession with contempt for life
We all need a sickness to live
A way to show our fear of Death
I've got hours of conversation trapped
Pages of words in lockdown
Video on double life
Doing forever
Don't end up in this place
—◦—

I made a mistake
I shouldn't have gotten so close to you
I won't be there for you
I'm not very good
I'm shallow and sick with Death
Soon will come the time you'll need me
I won't make it
I'll turn cold and speechless
You won't recognize me
You'll hate yourself for ever having said my name
—◦—

It's all important and meaningless
Depression drives a car into my back
It gets worse with time
Sometimes I can barely speak
The phone is almost impossible
I tried talking to a woman tonight
In the first 30 seconds I wanted to get off
Tour starts in a few days
Start the tour or kill me

At this point I'd take either one
━━♦

No more television
No more radio
Selected input
Must be careful to avoid the polluting leech
They call real life
I can't take the beatings like I used to
━━♦

There's a lot of prisons around here
━━♦

An important thing to learn:
There's times when it's better to shut your mouth
And listen to the other fool
━━♦

Humiliation is a great source for inspiration
Gets you out of bed in the morning
I shake my head from side to side
Rage comes through every pore
Re-wind the tape and remember the first time
The first time you felt the lump in your throat
You understood where all those mass murderers got off
━━♦

I've never seen Death so clearly
Two people I know dead in 3 weeks
I take Death seriously
Not life
━━♦

My eyes are shipwrecked
One more day in this shit
Anyone who can balance a checkbook
Is sick in the head and needs help
━━♦

Tonight I sat next to Hubert Selby
We read stories aloud in my room
I remember looking at his arm and hand
As he read about getting his ribs cut out of his body
He was just 18 and stranded in Germany
This man of such strength and clarity
Death hung around for hours after he left
Staring at the walls, sniffing the air

Getting lessons
On how to be that heavy
And not make it look like more than breathing
—

One of these days I'm going to get it right
See myself into extinction
I'm getting the blade sharper with the passing days
My focus is narrowing
I think Death is talking to me more now than ever
Wait until it comes down
—

Back in the hotel chain
Night off in nowhere
Thin Lizzy playing on the box
I can't find words to describe
How the fact that life repeats itself
Breaks my heart worse than anything I know
—

Full moon tonight
I walked down a street that lines the highway
I imagined I was doing an interview
Using the woman as a therapist
She asks me why I'm like this
I tell her that I'm fucked up
I don't wait to hear what she thinks
I want to shoot someone in the face
—

Watching the road pass
Death's steadying hand on my shoulder
The miles fill me with isolation
Facts that jam my throat shot
What a way to die
Neon and sand
Dead animals and hours
—

Letter from the stripper
They want to touch your body
They never get to
It makes them want to kill you
But their words and eyes leave scars
I could show you something else
Maybe you're too far gone

Too fucked up to feel anything
Besides strange disconnected bitterness
A hollow wooden gut that confuses your instincts
Maybe I'm just another man
Who wants to check your flesh and leave
I will fall short of all your expectations
—+

Maybe you could show me something different
I keeps seeing my brains on the ceiling
Don't try to love me
I'll just turn on you
I can't help it, it's what I do
I look so hard
I don't end up seeing anything
The whole world is empty to me
Everyone's reading from a script
No one's happy with their role
Show me something else
I'll try not to hurt you too much
—+

My mother is somewhere still breathing
She's in this room somewhere hiding
Telling me to kill myself
I don't forget a word
All the diseases she screamed into me
Her neurotic flailing rants
Whenever I fuck up
I emulate her
Whenever I backslide
I see her try to raise a son
That should have been terminated
A mistake walks
—+

All I see is Death now
Went to a diner today
All the people eating
Insects with skull masks
The food was tasteless
I think it won't be long now
I want to die in the desert
I can close my eyes and see the sun setting
I can feel the heat

Funny thing is that I'm not afraid
Mildly inconvenienced
I'll have to make some phone calls and tie things up
I'll have to talk about money
I'll have to disgust myself one more time
—◦

Death sits across from me
Death adds shade to the room
A heavy invisibility
Death makes music sound better
Death makes my eyes see through people
I have to wear a mask when I'm out amongst them
I have to use a different language to be understood
My true language is that of Death
My main line
—◦

What can you show me that won't make me leave you
What can you say that doesn't sound like a kick in the teeth
Is there a way you could touch me
And make me feel closer than 1000 miles away
Could you pull me out of the desert, out of the jungle
Could you take the taste of Death out of my mouth
The duration of a dream is all you get
The rest is so cold
These smoke filled rooms
These chicken lights
I smell the circus and head for the biggest tent
I amaze myself
I see how bad I need these strangers to help me
To watch me punish myself with my ragged truth
Could you give me something that wouldn't choke me?
I've never been to handle real life
—◦

I don't fit
I don't identify
Death?
Fine
—◦

Depression
Everything becomes hollow
Voices sound distant and brittle
I wait for tomorrow

Perhaps I'll wake up in a different place
Where I'll be able to deal with myself
—◦—

I take chances with silence
To be away from the animal wall
To be alone
Sometimes I go too far
I turn on myself And can't stop
I use every means of distraction available
Workaholic spasms
Wound up and pushing for Death
—◦—

Downward stare
Grey brown faded
Teeth clenched
Silent streak
—◦—

Mother
Don't put pictures of me on your wall
I don't want to be there with you
Don't work voodoo on me
Sharing your blood is bad enough
—◦—

Without lies
Truth is meaningless
Charisma in others
Allows us to temporarily forget
Death's steady approach
—◦—

Life neither remembers nor forgets
It is valueless to itself
It doesn't care about you
You see how easily it leaves the room
—◦—

At this point I reckon I'm clean
Stripped of youth's fat
Staring unflinching into the Abyss
I'm paralyzed there
Under the impression I'm flying
Tapping my bones for marrow
Thinking silently
And without the need to impress others

Life is the same always
It's the surroundings and their lure
That have become so serious
I bate my own trap
And wait for myself to walk in and trip the mine
—+

Focus
The fact of a blade
The fact of its sharpness
Steel cuts bone
Not love or hate
—+

Bones
Moon shining blue off bone
Hold someone so tightly their bones crack
After the flesh is burned and hacked off
It's down to the bones
After we've said all the bullshit
Love lines/romance/drama/compliments
After we've carved our way through the sex
Tried to give it meaning and failed in silence
After choking on life's putrid breath
A breath of grey room suicide and sun light vacancy
Let's take it down to the bones
I wonder what your skull looks like
I could cook your ribs in my oven
Your juice running down my face
A head bone in a million pieces
.45 in the face
Take me to a better place
Skeletons dancing and grinning
Shuffling on the floor of my room
Take the bones of all the dead Viet Vets
March'em down Pennsylvania Avenue
Send me the bones of my father
I'll beat my mother to Death with them
Break her arms with his arms
Skin the kid next door
Build a scarecrow with his bones
I want to see my teeth in a cup
My skull in my hands
I laugh with Death

I have no hope
—◦—

Lollapalooza
Today someone threw a bra onstage
I asked if someone had lost a garment
I didn't see any one raising their hand
I asked if there was a dead girl in the dirt
No one said anything
They could chop her into pieces
And instead of doing the rock thing with their lighters
They could cook her and save money on food
—◦—

The cars passed me
I watched their red lights rip across the black top
I was walking along some high way
I don't really know where I am tonight
Some hotel in Virginia
Most of the nights are like this
Alive and not sure where
The silence in this room is good
It's all I can take of them right now
Out there they want to know what's the matter
They have questions and they don't care about you
It's their noise that sets me on edge
Pulled into their lives
In the middle of tonight's nowhere
—◦—

You shouldn't have talked that shit
You leave me no choice but to wound you
Once I start I don't stop
Don't bother trying to talk to me
I'll only hurt you more
I don't try to help it
It's the part of me that lives to hurt
Walk away or I'll play with your mind
It's easy
It makes sense to hurt you
I think of you in your room crying
It warms my heart
I was the one you didn't win
One you couldn't control
Your beauty didn't impress

You idiot
Someone should lead you gently to the street
And shoot you between your ears
—

Many nights alone now
I like it better this way
I don't want to feel your touch
It's all bullshit
Whatever I touch I ruin
I have no regard, no need, no feeling
I feel stronger every day
—

I have pigs in my brain
Pigs in my face
Women pigs walking funny with their pants riding high
That big gun on their hip
Pigs with their stage costumes
Their little acts and dances
Sometimes I can't see why I'm with this shit
A lot of musicians remind me of intense child actors
Actors are the worst
They should be kept in camps, out of circulation
What human jokes
Keep me away from them
—

Final days of this tour
Winding down
Feels like summer camp coming to an end
I am confronted with feelings that I hate
I don't want to dwell on any of this shit
I have a feeling that I will though
Met too many good people on this one to forget soon
You can see some of the people wearing out
Stress is showing up and the cracks are getting bigger
Summer '91 drawing to a close
I wish we were doing another month of this tour
The sunset of my 11th summer on the road
I am filled with torn sadness
I keep it hidden
—

Lolla
The air is moist in Orlando FL

8.21.91 2:54 AM
The show let out at 10:15 PM
Denny's is still full
They watch me eat
I cash out and listen to the rednecks
Talk shit about people's hair
My head hurts from running it into a guitar
Cars beep and wave as I walk down Colonial Ave
The hotel is full of kids
They're drunk noisy and hanging out
How can you not like them
I don't know them
I don't want to know them
But I like them still
4 more shows to go
Makes me sad to see it slowly end
Seems like a long time since Phoenix
My brain dulled from 148 interviews in 5 weeks
I'm exhausted and I hate everything
I know one thing though
The day I'm flying home from Seattle
I'll wish we were in Phoenix
Doing it all over again
It's the nature of Motion Sickness

I tried to let the wall down and let you see me
I tried but the other one started talking
All I could do was listen to my voice talk you away from me
You're not the first one
It always happens
I think that some people don't fit and never will
They have to find a different way to get through it
It makes them look stupid and mean
Lost and reckless
To them, you're the one who's lost
I ran out of ways to deal with you
I ran out of shit to say to you
That's why I just stare and silently curse you

You would rather deal with someone who's not as real as pain
Someone who doesn't sweat as much
Someone quieter and more prone to all the normal bullshit

Someone that makes you feel superior
Life needs a little fakeness in it to make it easier to swallow
That's where the make-up smoke machines come in
I live in a different world
You will remember it as tragic
Painful and simple
I want to feel the muscle come off the bone
Exhaustion and insanity pound me
It's the reward and the punishment at once

Sometimes I have relapses
I think of you and my entire body weeps
I see your face on other women all the time
I'm alone in this room wondering where you are
I'll probably never see you again
After you, I feel cynical towards women
Guarded and defensive
I don't want to go through that again
I've learned about being alone
In recent weeks I've been doing it a lot and it's not so bad
I understand that there will always be distance
Between me and everyone else
I deal with it in silence

Where is the Highway Man tonight
Like the Ghost Rider
He can't stop moving
There's nothing back home
He tried it before
Found suicide waiting in the living room
He looks into the palms of his hands and counts the lines
Black with exhaust
Mind powered by exhaustion
He can feel and hear their bodies falling apart
The miles and the years pass by
You wonder what they see in their world
He took to the road instead
Chose movement and fury
Over stagnation and frustration
He's out there somewhere
Looking at the strangers in the roadside diners
Picking up legend with every minute he stays out there

It takes strength to stay out there
You have to be a little crazy too
You have to see the insanity of life and be able to handle it
Catch it but not get caught up in it
You see the ones that got caught up
They're dead already
—⊹

There's no night like tonight
They're all different
I went out there
I could taste the air
The power lines buzzing
I became part of the current
Like I knew exactly what was supposed to happen
So when the pig ran the stop sign
And nearly ran my ass over
My heart didn't skip once
I watch the man across the street watch me
He's plugged in too
We're both riding the current
It's not paranoia
It's just being on
Connected by the eyes
The eyes flash like knives
In the 7-11
I watch the man behind the counter
Try to lower the voltage of the drunk
Who's challenging his nationality
The drunk's eyes are glassed and out of control
He's ready to blow out
On the way back my entire body hums
I think that I'll never get far away enough from this
Do you ever feel the need to go somewhere
Forget everything so you can remember yourself?
You get a good way down the road and then the phone rings
Not tonight
A night for nights
Dried blood by the bus stop
A car patching out in the parking lot of the market
Where the hell could I go?
No, I'm plugged in
Hooked
—⊹

NJ hotel room
Why did I say the things I did
What was it that made me feel I needed you so badly?
I must have been insane
Now I'm far away from you and I don't miss you at all
I don't remember the time I spent with you
All I remember that was that I was uncomfortable
It wasn't your fault
Some people don't fit in
I'm convinced of it
Better now that I'm alone in some fucked room
The highway's outside and it's late at night
I'm dying alone
I don't have to explain a thing to anyone
The phone doesn't ring
The world is out there
So are you
So far away
I used to miss the touch of a woman
Long periods in which no one touched me
Now it's relief
To not desire women will be
A total triumph

LA should be remembered
For all the dead bodies
All the pretty girls
Faces torn and dragged by drugs
Suntanned drunks
The gallons of dried blood on the sidewalks
The bullet casings
The blank stares of the air-conditioned
Don't forget me
The one who wrote
Everything, Fear and Nothing
The pigs, real Death squads
We have it all!
Crack, Barbara Streisand
Compton, Westwood
Crips, fake tits
And Death
Lots of Death

Nobodys killing nobodys
Hiding the bodies nowhere
Someday they'll all get bored
And stop breathing
Until then
Keep low and keep rockin'
—❀

At some point I stopped
I saw what was there
I no longer had to live a lie
Loneliness is for the half blind
I feel sorry for 'em
Sitting in their rooms waiting
Walking the streets looking
Watching romance films hoping
Self inflicted cruelty
I broke off from that ride
I see the truth in the solitary mind
I don't love you
I'm free
I'm not waiting or fooling myself
I'm here
You can say anything you want
I've got vacant parking lot eyes
My thoughts are worn
Stacked like scrap in a heap
There's no difference between me
And 100 yards of chain link fence
You can talk to me
I've got stripped bolt ears
I've heard it all
And it all sounded the same
It twisted me up until I let it go
I'm as meaningless as the air in your lungs
It's all a Death Row isolation cell to me
Life
Straight no chaser
No raper reaper ripper or peeping tom
If I never see you again
If I sit this room and die
It'll be the truth
If I tell you I know you

And want to know you better
It'll be something else
—

Do you like me?
I like you
I think I do
I'm trying
I'm too fucked up for the rest of it
I have to go slow and lie to myself
Otherwise all I hear is my mother screaming
I can smell the cigarette smoke
Her screaming and things breaking
Some boyfriend leaving the house
It's all about fucking
That's as far as it goes
Past that I start to choke
I have contempt for any woman that likes me
I equate them with cruelty and my mother
I have doubts about any woman that wants to touch me
It never lasts long
A few times and then all I can think of
Is being by myself forever
It's a cycle that never ends
I learned it at home
—

Sometimes I find myself thinking about this woman
It hurts to know we're both alive right now
And that I'll never see her again
Tonight it got me
From out of nowhere
All of a sudden I was thinking of her
I have lied to myself enough
Convinced myself that it was better than it was
It's never been the same since
That much is true
The whole thing makes me sick
I don't want to be with women any more
They don't do anything for me
It's always the same wall
I was thinking that life is short
You think that someday you'll get it together
And the you realize

You're going to be one of those people
One of the ones you knew you would never turn out to be
You realize that people take this shit to the grave
And you feel like a damn fool
Something tells you to get up off your ass and move
That it will only get better if you do something
But if you have no idea what that is
Then you wander aimlessly through life
Able to get to and from work
Able to grow older
Finding you have this horrible ability
To be able to repress your feelings
Until even you forget you have them
To deny yourself
To be consumed with a pain so pure
That you really think it will drive you insane
To become a coward
And do your best to make it look like something else
Like acting brave
Bravery is the first sign of cowardice
Stoicism is two steps behind
I give myself the silent treatment all the time
It's the only thing that makes sense at this point
—◦—

In Death's Shoes:
Everything has meaning
Everything is meaningful
Everything is meaningless
Everything is mean
It all makes sense
-It's all bullshit
Death fucks love in the neck
Death makes me see the end
At the beginning of everything
Death makes me want to sleep
Death is a relief
Death is a release
Death is my master and inspiration
A good boss
A good reason to live
A great reason to die
Death is the only thing I know

That doesn't need an excuse
Death doesn't lie
Death is an equal opportunity destroyer
Carpe diem motherfucker

I was raised on a steady diet
Of hate, fear, intimidation racism
I felt strange all the time
My mother's boyfriends touched me
My mother screamed a lot
Kept me distant and on edge
Now I'm older
I've been called every name in the book
My heart is shallow
But sometimes I feel deeply in need for something
Something I won't be able to reject or abuse
Something I won't attach so much selfish protective fear to
Something I won't project endless hatred upon
A reason to live
I don't buy the rest
After what I've seen
Don't even try it
But I don't know what it is
I don't believe it exists
So when you talk to me
Keep your mouth shut

Hotel rooms
Bleeding moons
Nightly gunshot wounds to the head visit me
I look at the ceiling and fear sleep
A chain of dead mothers in the hall
Their bodies burnt and smoking
Endless fathers with hatchet notches on their necks
Dead women showing up in the corner of my eye
It's a slow moving horror
Darkness fills me
I'm choking

Kill mine
Kill them
I can't

I don't want their blood on my hands and face
I've tasted too much
I have enough of it in my body already
They hold me captive
Their blood keeps me here
Kill them
Burn them
Burn their houses
Their possessions
Make sure you get all the pictures of me
While you're at it burn all the other houses down
Burn all the streets
Incinerate the moon
Come into my dreams and smoke'em out
They'll lie and tell you they know me
Don't believe'em
Pull their fucking fingers off the chain link
Drag them away screaming
Smack them in the teeth
Kill them
Chop them up in their beds
Wrap his mouth around the exhaust pipe
Gas him in his own garage
Put her on a clorox diet
Make her tell you about the seminar
Light the planet on fire
The spectators can watch
From their fire escapes
After that come for me
I won't resist
I'll be expecting you
—◆—

Another night and all I can do is sit and be silent
Silence has become my life filter
I figure if you can't deal with them
Then deal with yourself
If you can't deal with yourself
Then do the best you can
Not to let time fool you into
Doing something stupid
Like living forever
Like giving in and stopping your heart

Like going to them
And looking for some part of yourself
I can tell you
It doesn't exist

Seeing devil's tails
I see'em twitch
In the corner of my eye
There's tunnels and hallways
Lines and chutes
The hallway to the back yard
That would have been the place to have shot him
With his own .38
To have seen his face
Pulling down three masks
Recognition, Fear and Relief
I walk down Death's tunnel
I can tell you what it's like
It goes at a slight downhill angle
It looks like it's always about to get bigger
And then it just gets smaller
Sometimes its tail is around my throat
Rooms become holding cells
People turn into garbage jokes
They offer me love
I give them back parts of their fingers
And 30 years of sharpened abuse
It sticks like jellied gasoline
And makes them just like me

Bring in your gods
Before they rust
Young man
Born
With holes in his pockets
Left to scream
On the Avenue
Pick a city
Any city

Silent terror disease
I don't speak human

I only scream
Machine number criminal
Soon they'll rape themselves
They'll stand in line
To fuck machines
Anything
To die clean

10 things to do with your parents remains
-Feed the homeless
-Make wallets, belts
-Props for a home movie
-Leave parts in restaurant bathrooms
-UPS to relatives for a visit
-Watch'em rot
I know that's only 6
I only thought them up
After I dumped their meat at Greyhound
Ok, that's 7

I like this only because

awsome

You're alive but in this room you're a ghost
The last few nights you have come to haunt me
It's 4:19 AM
The room's getting smaller
I think about what they did to you
I tried to make you see that I was different
Maybe you saw something I didn't see
Perhaps you saw them in my eyes
I'll never see you again
It's never been the same
I feel so fallen
So old and final
This night breaks Time's nose

4:46 AM, can't sleep
I think I did it wrong
All I know is
When you touch me
I think of watching those men
Fuck my mother

Prince charming got dragged

4 city blocks by his dick
She shone like a beacon
Decaying behind blood and urine colored glasses
10 princes left skidmarks the next day
She never moved an inch
What did you think she was going to do
She was only taught how to survive
Cruelty is all in your mind
So just don't think

Sad rituals
I think I'm above it all
Somehow got past, through or around it
I couldn't be more wrong
I accidentally punish myself
It keeps me busy
I don't know what else to do with time
I always have to be abusing something

I remember my mother's boyfriends
One in particular
Drives me into silence
Makes me want to sit in rooms
Clenched silence
Funny thing
Every night now I'm visited by Suicide
It's like an Armed Forces recruiter
I keep so much under the surface now
It's never been like this
A lot of things
I can't speak about out loud
Life haunts me now
Draws all the faces pale
When they talk
I know what they're talking about
And at the same time I have no idea
I feel like I'm going to slip and fall into a hole
Choke myself in a dream
Sometimes I wish I never happened

I miss you
I wish you never left me

ws me
this shit

οο now I don't know
I wonder where all this is going to end up
Can you make yourself so much of a fortress
That you can't get out
Because you've crushed the keys
Under the weight of your self hatred
—◦

Hey superman
Hey asshole
Hey Terminator, Mr. Action, Iron Man
You look hunted
Did you think you were something special?
Now all the assholes you spat on
Are running your life
They call your name and you come
All the shitheads know your name
You don't shine like you used to
You're not so slick
You look scared and old
Frozen with the shit still stuck to your smile
The dogs at your heels just ate your shoes
Ambition?
You never had any
You just wanted them to like you
So you could conveniently hate them
And now you'll do anything
To get them to give you a free breath
—◦

I lie to myself here in this room
My descending box
I make it up inside so I don't go insane
I lie to myself constantly
It makes life easier
I make up reasons to live
Fake romances
Dead parents
I never liked much anyway
—◦

Howard Johnson's right off the 80

Loneliness was outside my window tonight
I heard it's voice
It's the loneliest wail I ever heard
It was the sound of trucks roaring by
I lay in my bed and stared at the black hole ceiling
Loneliness clawed the glass again and again
I know better than to let it in
It always ends up staying too long
—

Sharks
There was a drive by shooting in the neighborhood today. In the store tonight a guy I know told me that there were some Bloods in the parking lot. They had been seen driving around looking for Crips. They ran their cars up and down my alley. The growl of their engines were predators stalking the cement. Out looking. Smelling blood sweat and fear. I sat in the dark and waited for the gunshots and the sound of frenzied rubber grinding garbage into powder.
—

The fire pulls the flesh back
The fire turns the flesh black
Light the fire
Burn it all night long
Call me up if you want some pain
Call me if you're tired of talking
And just want to scream
Hang them from light poles by the collar bone
Let me know when you're on fire
I'll be right over
Walk with Death all night long
Swing it
I see the fire in your eyes
If you want to see some of my blood
I'll show you
You gotta walk with Death
All the time
All the streets know your name
Can't you tell?
Swing Death like a watch on a chain
When you want to die
Call me
—

I would have swung from a chain of command

A chain of blood colored steel...
Your eyes meant that much to me
—⊕-

Please stay alive
I think about you coming down from that last tour
Wondering how you're making it
I never want to read about you overdosing in your room
I don't want to have to defend you to people that will talk shit
I would do it though
Always
So take good care of yourself
If you forget how
Call me
I'll remind you
—⊕-

Lost son walk alone through the autumn leaves
Think about if you had a friend
Would it be a he or a she?
What would you talk about?
Good not to be in prison
The rest sounds like leaves scratching the sidewalk
Lost son like you ever had a chance
You know the pain and silence
The long walks alone
Trying to retain sanity
So young and already so rusty
Buried for years
What happens when you finally explode?
Lost son whatever you do don't hang yourself
Don't get hung up on the words that they throw
They don't know what they're saying
They don't know anything at all
Lost son do you ever wonder when
Real life starts
Or did they pick pocket your mind
So you no longer know what life is?
Lost son look for me tonight
I'm lost and I can't see
All the bright lights
Have taken my eyes away from me
Lost son be careful out there
Those smilers are crooked

They'll fuck the taste right out of your mouth
—◦

Could you believe there's a man
Well known, recognized everywhere he goes
Compliments and accolades heaped upon him
He travels the world
Could you believe this man has enough self hatred
To constantly cripple himself with loathing
He makes records blah blah blah
He is deafened by applause
He feels no closeness to any human
He can't talk
He can't touch
He is depressed often
Not because he's a genius
Nor anything else so interesting or romantic
He's just fucked up
Don't tell him
Don't tell anyone
No one
Not a soul
—◦

Another woman gone
I can't talk to them
I get so close and then pull away
I've learned a lesson
The only reason I reached out in the first place
Was because I thought that's what you're supposed to do
Now I see that there isn't any such thing as supposed to
You go through life and rip holes in its skin
Then you die and the next fool is lined up
—◦

I live in the cult of the night
Go out there in the day time
You must be crazy
I did it today
It's like a war waiting to happen
Fuck that
Give me the night
Panhandlers and pigs
Gangs roving the streets
Night time in this neighborhood

Is like the deep black sea
Sharks, killers
Not a problem unless one of them is hungry
And then it's nothing but a problem

The nights pass over me
They hover above me
Silent specters
Bed cloth on top of me
I sweat underneath
Eyes of sadness upon me
I'm in the center of a flesh hurricane
The nights pull blades across my face
No one can see the scars
I can feel them though
This time around, life puts humps in my back
Makes me beg
Please
A feeding hand to bite
Until I feel bone stop my teeth
Tonight
Stop my mind from wounding me
Maybe you could somehow touch me
And not make me want to skin myself
I know about the Abyss
I could tell you stories about
Unending darkness
But then I'd see your stupid mute animal eyes
And all I'd want to do is break your fucking arms
And throw you off the balcony
Watch your meat hit the parking garage roof
And call it another night

Don't come close
I'll hurt you
It's all I know how to do
I can't translate the pain into words
That don't cause pain
Don't tell me you love me
You'll make me think of my mother
And 1000 broken windows
Years of knotted screams into the bed

So much hate it would break your ribs
I put the miles through my eyes
I slam silence into my brain
Anything to get away
Walk away from me as fast as you can
Never speak of me or to me again
It's too late
For all that
Death is the only shadow on my road

Men hugged him
Women asked him to come home with them
The money rolled in
He was so lonely it was pathetic
If they knew how he lived they would laugh
Sometimes he saw it all as punishment
Never escaping the humiliating inferno of his parents
The parents are gone now
Now he gets paid to humiliate himself
He constantly disgusts himself
In the name of telling the truth
Loneliness and alienation choke him
He tells people to stay alive
He tells himself to die

I live behind a wall of scar tissue
Scare tissue
Scarce issue
I don't like to think of myself
I like lifting those weights though
I like the feeling of pain
Nothing else
I am rescued from my mind
The nights are painful again
I can't do anything with that kind of pain
It's bad
Behind the wall of scar tissue
Hemmed in tight
I don't want them to know me
I tell them everything so there will be nothing left
That's the part I'll keep for myself
I figure the deeper I get into the pain

The better I'll be at dealing with it
That's how bad I hate this shit

100 women left me tonight
I didn't take it too well
I kicked myself for letting it matter
I kicked myself for letting it go so far
I lost myself in the shuffle
Now the room is cold
All of a sudden it's Saturday night
There's no magic
Too dangerous to go outside
No shit
I pride myself in being the loneliest man on earth
Damn

December 19 1991
Part of my life ended
My best friend was murdered
On my front porch
He never hurt anyone
The man who shot him in his face
Never knew his name
I am still alive
Sort of
From now on
My life is totally fucked and without purpose
Without inspiration
A mask that I will die wearing

After dark I wait for something horrible to happen
I figure I'll have people shooting at me for the rest of my life
Like a drama in installments
Nightmares delivered to my door
Darkness comes and I wait for more horror
I figure we'll be friends for life
I'm swimming in an animal bag
Everything smells like meat
Everyone is a killer
I look at all of them now
I search out their eyes
I let them know that I'll kill them back

They take one look and they know I mean it
I lock door behind me
Everything that moves begs me to attack it
I know how people are now
They take your money
Break your heart
Or try to kill you
Now I walk the streets like a secret animal
Some of them know
But not all of them
The one that fucks with me
Will lose his throat
He'll have no idea what he's fucking with
I live on the outskirts of humanity
I am scarred for the rest of my time here
That's all it is to me
Time left here
Time spent walking the city filth
Breathing in and out and keeping my teeth sharp
Waiting for something horrible to happen again

Every slow dance took my breath away
Pinned my heart to the wall
I believed every slow song
I was intoxicated by the smell and the movement
Every one of them broke my heart a little
Now there's nothing but wise bitterness
Fatigue from seeing the whole thing
The pool of blood in the dirt
The end of real time has begun
It's all legendary from here

The detectives went through my house for hours
I was at the pig station
I didn't know until later
They went through the food in the kitchen
I got back to the house and all kinds of shit was turned over
My best friend's blood was all over the front walk
They're looking for something to bust us for
The pieces of shit even went through the attic
They were curious as to why I had so many tapes
He talks to me and makes me think he's my friend

I look at him and know he thinks I'm scum
If I give these pieces of shit the time of day then they win
You know
There's so many pieces of shit in the world
It's amazing anyone gets by
The pigs asked if me and Joe were faggots
They were so relieved when they found out we weren't
Fuck you pig
Like I have to prove myself to you
I can't think of a more fucked up situation
I have to talk to these shitheads all the time now
They still ask other people about me
Like I might have been up to something
I'm some kind of suspect?
Nah, but you sure are some kind of pig

Joe you should have seen the tabloids talk about you
They really love the fact
That your father was married to the bitch in Charlie's Angels
They talk about her sorrow
How you two were so close
Like you hung out all the time
How you were 29 and in Black Flag
One of your father's piece of shit friends was lying
Talking a lot of shit
You looked great in the Enquirer
Good pictures of you and what ever the fuck her name is
I saw her at your wake
I wanted to spit on her
Your father had it at Gazarri's
All his AA friends were there
After all these fake ass people who didn't know you
Had spoken and congratulated themselves on their acting
And talked a lot of shit about god and AA
Your father stood at the end of a line
So people could come up and talk to him
Your mother didn't know anyone there
She just stood to the side
With her husband and your step-sister
They weren't used to the Hollywood sickness
It was gross
After that we went and looked at your body

Your father didn't go
He didn't go to your funeral either
Don't know why
Maybe because there would be too many people
Too busy with their own grief
To compliment him on his
I miss you man
I look at pictures of you and I can't take it
Yesterday I wanted to crawl inside the pictures and be with you
I have been thinking a lot of dying myself lately
Life is pretty boring without you around
I have to tell you Joe
I did it all for you
I was hoping that if I went out there and did something good
You would see that you could do something magnificent
Like I told you the night before you died
You have such a great talent
It's because you didn't lie
I admire that truth
You will inspire me for what's left of my life
I see now that it might not be all that long
That piece of shit took you out
In less time than it takes to turn off a light
When I was looking at you on that gurney
That bullet hole in the side of your head
All filled in with mortician's clay
All the powder burns on your face
What courage you have to be dead like that
This thing that we all fear the most
And there you are pulling it off like it's nothing
You even had a slight smirk on your face
But you were cold and you smelled like formaldehyde
It was so hard to leave that room with you in it
It took me 3 times I think
I kept coming back to say something else to you
It never seemed to be enough
It will never be enough
Please come visit me in a dream soon
I miss you so much
My good friend

1992 is a couple of hours away

I'm staying in someone's house
I am almost 31
All my stuff is in storage
I am single and plan on staying that way
To appeal to the more tender nature of a woman
Is a total waste of my time
What a joke
Meanest damn people I ever met
I am alone in the world and there's no changing that
My loneliness burns deep within
I don't mind because
I am one from none
My line has never been so clean cut
Death has stripped most of the words from my speech
Talk is a disease
Action is its cure
Death has been walking with me all year
Talking to me in the night
I answer with my insomnia
Paranoia has put a hard shine in my eyes
I mix humor with my fury
Efficiency with my alienation
Beauty with my rage
The rising sun is my silent battle cry
Exhaustion is my victory
Death is that which I measure myself by
I acknowledge no peer or ally
I understand Death as master
And the definition of absolute power
My path is clear and laid out before me
The wind rushes past me
I dream of empty desert landscapes
And proceed forward

Handwritten annotations:

happiness
sorrow Numbers
guess slowly

Feeling ur ya emotion
Dealing w/ your emotion
Not dealing w/
any
Depression
Anger,
extreme
sadness
insanity
if you
let it
control
you

(words are not enough for my thoughts)
m.c.